Leaving the Bubble – Into Blue Depths: Intriguing Insights from Giving Up a Career for a Life as Scuba Diving Instructor

Sebastian Geese

Bibliografische Information der Deutschen Nationalbibliothek: Die Deutsche Nationalbibliothek verzeichnet diese Publikation in der Deutschen Nationalbibliografie; detaillierte bibliografische Daten sind im Internet über http://dnb.dnb.de abrufbar.

Herstellung und Verlag: BoD – Books on Demand, Norderstedt

ISBN: 978-3-7543-2129-4

Preamble

For many years I have had the dream to write a book, but never did so as I was lacking inspiration for what to write about... That was until I went on one of the greatest adventures of my life so far by quitting my well-paid job and moving to Ibiza and Thailand for a few months each and working as a scuba diving instructor. By doing so I achieved a dream and goal which I had held and notoriously worked towards for several years, a dream that had always been accompanied by romantic and idyllic pictures of living a glorious life on the beach. When I decided to go on this adventure, it did not take long until an idea for a book manifested in my mind, but in the end this whole trip and these pages have become so much more than I intended them to be.

What started as a dream of an extended break and a possibility to achieve mindfulness and peace of mind again, has moved beyond taking a break from life and has become an eye-opening and life-changing experience in many regards. Therefore, it is no surprise that what was planned as a book about the more practical experiences and tips has turned into a reflection on some of the deeper and more fundamental insights which I gained during my almost twelve months outside the rat race of the corporate world. While I had a rough outline in mind when I started gathering the first bullet points and thoughts on the beach of Ibiza, it was as much about the process of writing a book as it was about having the outcome in the end. After all, it turned out as a powerful tool and means not only to help me reflect and digest on my experiences along the way, but also to remind me of the good times I had and resharpen my spirit related to the insights I gained, when I was typing up the final pages back in my apartment in Germany. I am almost certain that without my regular work on this book I would have been sucked back into the corporate rat race much more and faster than I anyways have been after a few months.

These pages are probably also a perfect example of the non-importance of a specific location or certain infrastructural conditions for being productive and getting work done. I started gathering the first bullet points in my room in a dive center on the beach in Ibiza and typed the first lines somewhere high up in the air between Frankfurt and Dubai on my way to Koh Tao. While the endless coffees or breakfasts in cafes on the beach of Koh Tao or a café in the loud and hectic city center of Saigon are probably some of the more comfortable places I used to write in Asia, a loud café next to the pier in Koh Samui waiting for my ferry back to Koh Tao was probably one place where focus was among the hardest to achieve. There have been endless hours in my girlfriend's flat in Stockholm as well as my own apartment in Germany, but also summer houses around the Swedish south coast or somewhere in the middle of the Baltic sea on a ferry between Rostock and

Trelleborg. And if there is one lesson I learnt along the way, it is the one that for being creative and productive it does not require much more than motivation and a computer. And looking back in all honesty, the less comfortable and more messy places have usually been the most inspiring ones.

There is one thing I want to get clarified before diving deep into my experiences I made during one of the greatest years of my life. Even though I lived a somewhat privileged lifestyle for one year, this was in no way facilitated or enabled by a privileged background of some kind. Neither do I come from a rich background nor did I live the year on society's terms. It was only about making the right arrangements, being ready to take some risks and knowing when the time to step off had come. It turned out for me that it is much more about the right paradigms and principles than it is about the right background. Therefore, this book is going to be a story about everything being possible in life, not letting us be held back by imaginary restrictions and last but not least memories from a journey which was planned as a once-in-a-lifetime adventure but then turned into an eye-opener and game-changer towards a better and more meaningful life.

Table of Contents

1 Introduction 11

2 The Itinerary 17

3 Greatest Doubts and Excuses 29

   3.1 Finances 31

   3.2 Friends & Family 37

   3.3 Career 41

   3.4 Being Afraid to Fail 51

4 Intriguing Insights 59

   4.1 Make Your Life Lean to Make it Complex 62

   4.2 Spend Your Life Being Instead of Doing 74

   4.3 Happiness Will Not Find You 98

   4.4 Take Full Ownership of Your Life 120

   4.5 Being Introvert in an Extrovert Life 151

5 Leaving Fast Lane vs. Achieving My Mission 175

6 Settling Back Into "Normal" Life 186

7 Conclusions 193

8 Final Tips and Tricks 202

1 INTRODUCTION

I am writing these lines 30'000 feet above the ground, somewhere between Dubai and Kuala Lumpur, from where my next flight will take me to Bangkok. While flying has become a not to be ignored part of the normal life of millions of people, the purpose of my trip does still scare me a bit. It is probably not the only reason that I am flying on a one-way ticket, but also the adventure and life dream that underlies this whole trip. This is a book about fulfilling ones' dreams, not allowing your environment to hold you back from living your life to the fullest, the path that leads you back towards your true inner values and aspirations – and finally a story that shows how each decision and step in your life can act as a trim tab and enable an entirely different life at some point in the future.

My trim tab has been my Open Water Diver course in 2008. I was a university student, and it was during our exchange semester in Australia, when a friend of mine and I faced the question how to spice up our time down under and get some lasting memories. Naturally, there were two possibilities, which crossed our minds right away, learn to dive or learn to surf. My life would look vastly different today if we had gone for the latter.

Never ever would I have imagined in 2008 that a few years later I would have progressed from novice to inspiring students towards a life underwater myself. In fact, my diving career was far from promising in the years to come. Just recently did I check my logbook just to get confirmation for the sad fact that I had done 16 dives in 2008 and 2009, but no more until late 2015. Looking back on my life with the aspiration to be honest and tough on myself, there are two reasons why I did not dive for such a long time despite always longing to descend into blue depths again. One of them is an actual reason, the second has to do with procrastination.

Dealing with the fact that I wasted six years, in which I could have dived and progressed my diving career a lot, is easy when I blame it on being a student, who had other things on my mind and lacked the funds to really engage in a – let's face it – expensive hobby like diving. It is certainly a part of the reason. However, being honest on myself, I need to acknowledge that procrastination played an important role as well. All divers are trained to the principle to always dive with a buddy. A buddy is exactly what I lacked, since for several years I could not motivate my friend, who I had done my Open Water Diver course with, to go diving again. And it took me exactly those years until 2015 to work up the guts not to make myself dependent on one buddy, but to finally take responsibility for my life and to look for buddies and join a diving club. In the end, it took me to finish my studies and to realize that I needed a new life goal, when graduation from university as my greatest goal so far had been accomplished. And so the rally began and the moment I joined my local dive club became part of my personal history as a moment drastically changing my future life.

I do not remember exactly what triggered this idea and how exactly it appeared back then, however after only a few dives after my break an idea crossed my mind... "I want to become one of those legends that inspired me so many times and become a scuba diving instructor and live abroad for a while myself". Having thought about it many times by now, I can conclude that the longing for a meaning behind diving for the pure fun of it and the pressing need for a new goal in my life were what was motivating me to put efforts into stepping beyond recreational diving and following a professional career path. In the end, I am in many regards a person who needs to see my own "aurora borealis" at the end of the paths that I am following and a deeper meaning behind my daily actions. And so it happened that I had finally found a new life goal for myself.

It still strikes me how much I underestimated my progress towards becoming an instructor respectively overestimated the time to become one. Having worked in project management for several years, I developed a habit to draw timelines and plans for everything I want to accomplish and so I did. Depending on which training agency you chose to go ahead with, you need about 60 dives and get certified in five specialty disciplines before you can attend the Divemaster program, one of the last steps before being qualified to sign up for the Instructor

Training Course. My – what I thought to be ambitious – timeline planned for 20 dives and one specialty course per year, which would have resulted in a minimum of five years. However, without even putting extraordinary effort into it, I found myself doing 70 – 80 dives and several specialty courses in the first year, so that I accomplished my first intermediate goal and became a Divemaster two and a half years later, just to finish the Instructor Training Course less than a year later despite being held up by medical issues. What can one learn from this experience? I for my part concluded that one of the greater mistakes, one can make in life, is not to dare to dream big and to underestimate our capacity to accomplish our dreams and goals, no matter how big, unachievable or far in the future they seem to be. In the end, it is passion, motivation and discipline that make the difference between achievement and mediocracy, while the two latter one stem a great deal from the first and seem to be there naturally if you are really passionate about what you are doing or want to achieve.

There are certain expectations attached to everything we dream of and everything we do in life. What did I expect from living in a remote sunny tropical paradise? It was on one hand what I had admired when being surrounded by Divemasters and Instructors on so many vacations before… I dreamt of a glamorous life always being surrounded by happy people passionate about what they do, a fun and relaxed time with sunshine year-round and an increased attraction to people of the opposite sex. Ultimately, I hoped that my sabbatical would reconnect me with my true values, help me to rest more in myself and become a more positive and inspiring person – all of which had somehow gone down the drain after living in my self-contained bubble for several years… a bubble that consisted primarily of spending more than eight hours a day in an neon-lit office doing a job that I had come to hate more and more, and spending the remainder of my time on things that had become habit or seemed to be expected from me by the people around me rather than the things I really cared about.

When I noticed that my thoughts started to become more and more negative, it had become urgent to take action and leave my toxic environment for the better. Even though I had to push myself to do it now or never and had to be tough on myself not to invent excuses, it finally turned out to be much easier to go the big step than I thought. It probably helped that I had already increased the number of people I talked to about this plan, as it is somehow the more difficult to step back from a plan the more people know about it. Once the journey had begun, it could hardly be stopped anymore and even now that it is still underway, I can already see the tremendous positive impacts on my life and personality, as will be explored in greater detail later in this book. Many of these impacts did already become apparent in the first leg of my adventure, but those who read on might already suspect in chapter 2 that it did not take me to full satisfaction yet, as I would otherwise not have written the first lines 30'000 feet above the ground, somewhere between Dubai and Kuala Lumpur.

Life is probably as much a journey as identifying your true values and principles is. It is quite probable that the latter takes a lifetime, and one might argue that it is not even meant to end at a certain time. There was one major decision to be made when I left my old life behind and started my journey. I had to make up my mind if I wanted to set a time limit and negotiate with my employer that I would return at a pre-defined date. The negotiation was cut short right from the beginning. I had already made an agreement to work as scuba diving instructor for a six months' season, while the maximum time my employer would keep my job would have been two months. As counterproductive as this may sound, I did happily accept it, as I was prepared to leave my job anyways and I was not thrown into temptation to stay in a job that had started to drain a lot of my motivation and energy. So, it happened that I found myself on an aircraft to Ibiza at the beginning of May 2019 and the only thing I knew was that I would fly out of Ibiza at the end of October or beginning of November. However, I insisted to me and others that I did not yet know if I would return to my old life by then or embark on the next leg of my journey instead... a wise choice as I was confirmed later during my journey!

My original dream was quite different than the actual journey, fortunately as I recognized while I was in my first job from May to October 2019. For several years I had been dreaming of working onboard a cruise ship as a diving instructor. I envisioned living the glorious life, cruise ship passengers experience, for several months, changing between amazing places regularly and being surrounded by happy guests and passionate colleagues. It did not happen due to a small detail.

By the end of 2018 I had a work contract of a major cruise ship operator on my desk, ready for my signature, as well as a specific date and port of embarkment to go on board. Timing was the only problem. Due to me becoming an instructor only in November 2018 and my notice period in my old job I would not have been able to go onboard before February 2019, a time by which the destinations with popular diving – Caribbean and South East Asia to name it – had already been staffed. Joining one of these would only have been possible, if I had worked up the guts to quit my old job before joining my Instructor Training Course in November 2018. As risk averse as I was, I considered that no option... In retrospective it would have been a wiser choice to take the greater risk, but not for the sake of ending up on a cruise ship.

When I sat on that aircraft to Ibiza in May 2019, I still considered it an option to work on a cruise ship afterwards. What prevented this from happening in the end were the working conditions on such cruises. As naïve as I was, I kept on believing that working 12 hours a day and seven days a week for six months straight would be great as long as you do what you like.

However, working eight hours a day and six days a week in Ibiza taught me an entirely different lesson.

As much fun as scuba diving still is for me, as much direly needed was the Sunday off. Even though it was a different way of looking forward to the weekend than in my old office job, physical exhaustion and working in tourism as an introvert still requested their tribute. After working in Ibiza for almost six months, I direly needed my well-deserved rest, because one day off per week had not been enough for a full recharge of my energy level. One can now easily imagine what six months without a single day off would have done to my physical and emotional state.

Consequently, I returned from Ibiza a little bit wiser now knowing more about being an introvert in an extrovert job. Luckily, I had found out early enough, so that I made the right arrangements and did not go for cruise ship after all. Even though I now argue that quitting my job before my Instructor Training Course would have been a better life choice, exactly this mistake – if one wants to call it like that – prevented me from going a step that I would have regretted rather sooner than later. As there is a countless number of interdependencies between all the decisions we take in life, it is impossible to see all their impacts. Yet it is imperative to take decisions in order to avoid a life in mediocracy. I will reflect a bit deeper on this later in this book.

What were my reasons to choose Ibiza over Thailand or another exotic place? The more I look back and the more I think about it now, the more I get to realize that after all it was just me being scared of taking a too big step out of my comfort zone and entirely leaving my bubble behind. Back at the end of 2018, when my decision for a destination was due, I was of course arguing entirely different. I kept on telling myself and others that I preferred Ibiza over other places because of the high lifestyle in a developed western country and the resulting possibilities to live your life outside of diving. I was proven wrong very soon, when I realized that I got to spent most of my time with colleagues and guests from the dive center anyways and, not a surprise, the native population was living separate from the temporary workers. Now sitting on the beautiful beach of Koh Tao it hurts to confess that there is actually more life outside of diving over here, so I took my initial decision based on false assumptions and could have gotten way more out of it, if I had not been afraid of the big leap that Thailand seemed to be back in 2018.

However irritating this insight is, there was one big advantage of Ibiza though, one that I only started to appreciate when I started to organize for Thailand and was able to compare – the benefits of the European Union! Free movement, health insurance, social security and permission to work in whatever member state are only a few to be mentioned. Sometimes it takes to see the other side to appreciate what you have been taking for granted almost your entire life.

As I am writing these lines on the beach of Koh Tao, it should become very obvious that these first six months of my journey had not been as fulfilling as I wished, since I would otherwise probably be back in my old life by now. If I had returned home after the first six months, I would very likely feel the desire to break loose very soon again. Now, however, after having been here for two months, it feels right to go home in a few months to embark on new adventures.

In November 2019 I spent 18 days at home, in between returning from Ibiza and boarding my flight to Thailand. This turned out to be the weirdest period of my entire sabbatical. When I booked my flights, it sounded great to spend a certain time at home. I would be seeing my friends again and would have enough time to get everything arranged for Thailand. I was even doubting if 18 days would be enough. It was, however, only a matter of days to get everything arranged and it was intriguing to realize how little most people cared that I was only home for two weeks between two legs of what felt for me as the greatest journey and adventure of my entire life. Many of them turned out to be so heavily stuck in their day-to-day affairs that conversations were so much more about the random topics I escaped from in the first place rather than being interested in what I had experienced and what would be next. It almost felt as if people were afraid of even only thinking and talking about topics that are outside the bubble that is called their life.

Consequently, it did not take long until I started to feel bored and stuck in what I had called my life before leaving and I started to wonder if I should have spent less time at home in between. Having been surrounded by inspiring, enthusiastic and full-of-life people for six months, it was painful to realize how mediocre my old life had been. Thus, I was direly waiting for November 18th and boarding my flights to Thailand, even though I anticipated by this time that a way bigger blues and crisis would hit me upon my return to Germany after however many months in Thailand. I expected it to be like the time after graduation from university, when I had found myself without a purpose, as my goal of graduating had been achieved. At that time, it had been a great relief to start working towards my goal of becoming a scuba diving instructor and working abroad for a while. It is therefore probably not a big surprise that identifying a new life goal or a next step played an important role in me getting ready to set a date for my return to Germany, as the reader will learn more about a few lines down this chapter.

So it happened that I found myself on a flight from Frankfurt to Kuala Lumpur, when I was writing the first lines of this book and have by now been living my life as a freelance scuba diving instructor on the island of Koh

Tao for two months, something that I would not even have dared dreaming about several years ago. In fact, even when I had set for myself the goal to do this for a while, there was one of my inner voices that kept telling me that I would not do it anyways.

It is quite interesting to look back and realize how differently I arranged my time in Ibiza and my time in Koh Tao. Having worked my entire professional life in project management, I am used to setting targets, drawing timelines as well as defining and implementing action steps, each of these actions having its own due date and contingency plan in case it does not work out. Sadly enough, this had influenced my entire mindset into a direction that I was also writing ambitious to-do-lists for every hour of my free time, squeezing more into a day than I could get done and seeing everything I did – even enjoying a dinner with friends – as yet another box to tick off. After all, it was probably also that project manager inside me who chose Ibiza. I had my work contract signed months before my flight, I knew I would work Monday to Saturday and how much I would earn and, ultimately, I knew from day 1 how long I was going to stay.

This setup sounded great and the project manager inside me was celebrating it big time. However, it came with big costs assigned to it. In life there are many decisions to be taken and preferences to be set, while the outcomes of each decision depend to some extent on universal principles and interdependencies or – as we might also call them – paradigms. One of them is that you can either treat security for freedom or you can treat freedom for security. Increasing one very likely sacrifices the other to a certain extent. I chose to prefer security when I decided to go to Ibiza, a mistake as I found out later.

At the time when I was still dreaming of becoming a scuba diving instructor, I was dreaming of the great freedom that would come with – the great freedom that would come with waving my old life goodbye and leaving the 9-to-5 scheme, which I had been trapped in for so many years, behind. Essentially, I had pictures in mind of me wandering the most beautiful beaches of the world in slippers and shorts. Reality hit me hard soon. As great as it was to live on the beach of Ibiza, as irritating was the insight that I had become less free than I was in my project manager life. I had to work six instead of five days per week, every single minute of the work day got planned and written on paper by our manager, management was telling us when to take days off and asking for additional days off felt like asking for absolution. The setup for Koh Tao was entirely different and got me countless sleepless nights the weeks before my flight to Thailand but turned out to provide much greater satisfaction. This time I chose to sacrifice security for the sake of freedom.

All I had arranged this time was a place to live and a pile of CVs in my suitcase. Neither did I know if and where I was getting work nor did I know how long I was going to stay, not even thinking of having a return flight booked. The decision to go all-in and try my luck freelance provided me with a great deal of freedom, but it took me a long time to accept the uncertainty and inability to plan, as it arose from this freedom. It felt great though. It enabled me to live in the moment rather than unconsciously counting down the days until November from the moment I arrived in Ibiza.

After all, that is what life is about. As humans in the 21st century, we have been socially conditioned to spend our lives doing instead of being. We are always striving for the next steps in our life, for the next accomplishment, a bigger car, the next life step of our kids or are eagerly waiting for our next vacation, if not even retirement. We are so busy doing this that we miss out on many of the magical moments, which life has to offer along the path. Life can only unfold its entire beauty if we allow things to happen and allow life to drive us within certain boundaries, for which we need to define how narrow we want to set them. We need to be ready for and allow ourselves to go with the flow. Life is so much more about enjoying the journey and indulging in the moment than about heading towards a certain point. For that to happen we must, however, learn to be comfortable to give up control for the sake of happiness.

Breaking loose from my old life caused me a major challenge to overcome. I had to start taking full ownership of my life. While it was easy to rest in the well-established structures and routines of my 9-to-5 job, my long-kept apartment and graved-in-stone social environment, I could not rest on my accomplishments anymore, when I arrived in Thailand. I had to get to know new people, find work where there were no vacancies published and find to myself again. We improve with every challenge we face though and, thus, it is no surprise that my sabbatical came with many valuable insights and positive personality developments, as I will reflect on in detail later in this book. One of the greatest outcomes though is that I changed from doing to being. I started being myself rather than spending my time fighting through the to-do-lists that I had made my very own cage in my old life. So, after all, it turned out to be the right insight during my time in Ibiza that I should not give up my real dream and should not be afraid of going all-in by going to Thailand. It took me six months though to realize this and be ready to take my second leg out of the comfort zone as well.

As mentioned earlier, when I embarked on my journey, I quit my job and all I knew was that I did not want to return into my old life. It only took one month of my time in Ibiza though, until an unexpected development made me face a major decision to take. A company, which I had without success applied for in the past and which I still considered an appealing employer, approached me if I would still be interested in working for them and starting the process of getting to know each other. There I had my dilemma. On one hand, I was by far not ready to think about the time after my sabbatical, inconceivable to arrange myself a new job. On the other hand, however, this sounded as too great an opportunity to refuse. Fortunately, the company faced no hurry to hire someone and showed understanding for my situation, so that procrastinating the decision got easy.

As with every procrastination in life though, the point in time will come that a decision must be taken and can no longer be procrastinated. So, it happened that I had a ready to be signed work contract in my hands and December 31st as a deadline for my decision. It, however, happened that by the end of 2019 I still struggled to take my decision for two reasons. Not surprising, the two weeks after Christmas turned out to be my most successful time, as they are the peak season for young adults to travel to South-East-Asia and take diving courses. Consequently, I found myself living my dream and having arrived where I always wanted to be, teaching course after course and getting to know countless interesting and inspiring people.

Of greater importance, however, was my dire desire for a new purpose in my life, since as elaborated earlier my long-term purpose of becoming a scuba diving instructor had vanished. I knew already by this time that going back into a 9-to-5 job in the place, where I had lived for years, would provide me financial stability, but by far no fulfillment and satisfaction. Even worse, it would feel like missing my sabbatical as an opportunity to change my life for the better. Fortunately, a vision for my future started emerging in the early days of 2020, getting me ready to sign the work contract that I had been procrastinating for long. As expected, it was a sad moment to realize that I had now set a definite end date for my sabbatical. What made this blues possible for me to handle was the insight that it was not going to be the end of my journey, but only one more necessary step towards my bigger goal, which the reader will learn more about towards the end of this book.

So, here I am now not being able any longer to deny the fact that my sabbatical will come to an end. However, it feels good now that I have an idea of what comes next.

It was back in 2015 when the idea of becoming a scuba diving instructor appeared in my mind. It did not take long, however, until doubts and excuses entered the stage as well. Very too often they go hand in hand with any great ideas and hold us back from achieving our full potential and living our life to the fullest. What will my friends and family say? Will it not ruin my entire career and pension savings? What if I fail to make it a success? These are just a few of the doubts and excuses that kept on appearing on my mind more often than helpful.

It is in our own hands to determine whether we live an outstanding or mediocre life. In everyone's life it takes a few major decisions to determine which path we follow. Safe paths to mediocracy, however, include the wide-spread traits of being afraid to step out of one's comfort zone and holding our environment responsible for how we live our life. When we look at it honestly, it is easy to understand why many people choose to hold their environment responsible for how their life goes. Using one's family background or economic circumstances, for instance, as excuses is way easier than accepting the fact that we could have done something different to be in a different situation now. Nobody is happy to admit that they did something wrong.

What differentiates humans from animals, however, is our self-awareness. While animals are driven by instincts, humans possess the unique trait of knowing their interests and passions and have the unique ability to determine the direction of their future life. Thus, it is our very own responsibility to let go of the reactive approach to blame our circumstances and take full proactive ownership of our life. Replacing the common phrase "I cannot, because…" by the as simple phrase "I will…, no matter what it takes" is by far not as easy as it seems but can make a tremendous difference in how our life goes.

After living a mediocre life for way too long and letting excuses hold me back, without admitting it, I now decided to not allow them to take over, as I did not want to look back some years into the future with the dire regret that I gave up my dream. What certainly helped me in times of doubt was to mention my plans to as many people as possible, as everyone you mention your plans to makes it more difficult to step back. After all, I kept procrastinating increased senses of commitment until the end, from delaying the acceptance of my job in Ibiza to delaying the purchase of my flights. I must confess that this whole trip scared me big time, so that only once I had booked my flights, it felt that I had passed the point of no return and would now do it.

So, let us look at which areas of my life caused me the greatest doubts and excuses and how they turned out in the end. Most likely not a big surprise, what caused me most sleepless nights at the beginning of 2019 were the impacts on my finances, social environment, and career. As one might already suspect and get confirmed, if reading on, the impacts were negligible, if not even non-existent.

3.1 Finances

In many western countries it still prevails as a paradigm these days that our life can be separated into four strictly distinct phases – childhood, adolescence, work life and retirement. It still prevails as a socially acceptable norm that our life must be linear, acknowledging a working career as the only reasonable way forward after adolescence and finishing our education. Living our life and enjoying our time is according to many people's standards supposed to be done in childhood, early adolescence and after retiring, while taking side-tracks or leaving the rat race for a while is often referred to as lazy or irresponsible if not even as a scrounger living on society's contributions. While I was getting ready to leave for Ibiza, it felt obvious that besides envy another feeling was present in some people – objections against living outside the socially acceptable standards. As such it was one of the milder and to some extent even a reasonable concern by some people if exiting the system for a while will not ruin my entire pension savings.

Trading our time for money is a common concept. Most of us spend about 40 to 50 years of our life selling our time in return for money, many of which hate their jobs and direly wait for reaching the legal retirement age. This has also been the case for me the last months before I left my job and embarked on my journey. The simple question, which we must ask ourselves, is whether we only want to trade our time for money or if trading money for time for a certain period can also be a legit approach. After all, the financial impact of taking a side-track for a year turned out negligible, which makes the entire discussion a philosophical one.

In the end the question is not if we can make it happen, but rather if we want to make it happen and how. We need to ask ourselves the simple, yet difficult to answer, question if we want to live our entire life saving for our pension or if we want to live in the here and now. In different terms it is essentially the question if we want to leave all the fun for later, when our body suffers impacts from a long and hard work life or if we want to have part of the fun now, when we are still young, fit and enthusiastic. Having been raised in a more traditional and conservative environment, my childhood and adolescent life conditioned me to save the fun for later, so it came as a great mind changer and relief when I decided to go for the latter. It is a simple thought that triggered this paradigm change.

Direly waiting for reaching the legal requirement age is intricately linked to doing a job, which we do not like. If, however, we do a job we like, there is no reason to not work a bit longer when we are old, if in return we can squeeze in some extended breaks as mini retirements along the way. It is the simple idea to distribute work and fun equally over our entire life span instead of working now in order to live later, but eventually not being able to enjoy our post-work life due to health problems or even not making it there at all. I do not have scientific proof but am convinced nevertheless that enjoying our life now increases the chance of remaining mentally and physically fit later. It is for sure, however, that doing something we like can also give us a purpose beyond the legal requirement age.

It did not take me long to answer the philosophical question if I wanted to make it happen. When I am now, nine and a half months into my journey and one and a half months before returning home, looking back, I am convinced that everyone can make it happen. I am even going so far to say that this one-year adventure will have a positive financial impact in the long term. After all, the critical exercise, which one planning a year off must go through, is to make one's life lean.

When preparing to go to Ibiza, I went through all my fixed costs to check which ones I could freeze or cut. The result was mind-blowing. Without much effort I instantly identified 55% of my costs, which could be cut or frozen and it could have easily been 87% if I had not decided to keep my apartment at home. To put it into the right perspective I must admit that this cut also included some insurances and pension funds, so I would not be able to keep my life that lean forever. The impact on these pension funds is, however, negligible and a simple simulation shows that I can easily keep a 10% reduction, when returning home despite reactivating all insurances and pension funds. It was an interesting exercise to identify how much unnecessary expenses I had accumulated over time. A little amount here and there, each of them not making a big difference, but over time the amount of wasted money to make a mediocre life bearable becomes significant.

After nine and a half months it is with a good degree of confidence that my year outside the rat race will cost me approximately 4,000 Euros, an amount that can easily be spent on a memorable vacation of two or three weeks. However, as the reader will find out in the next chapter, I will not be the person that I was before my adventure, as it will have developed my personality much more than two or three weeks of vacation ever could. As such those 4,000 Euros appear a well invested amount, even more so when considering that I did still live a good life and could have spent less if living a simpler life.

Going the next step of the equation delivers an even more mind-blowing result. If I assume that a fixed cost base reduction of 10% remains after returning home, I will reach break-even after less than two years, meaning that less than two years after one of the greatest times of my life a positive long-term financial impact will be realized. I would probably not have gone through the exercise to make my life lean, if I had stayed in my old life. Without breaking loose, it is way too easy to stick with old habits, if there is no financial pressure to change anything. This simulation, however, considers that I kept my apartment at home. Comparing my monthly rent with the 4,000 Euros mentioned above, it becomes apparent that there would not have been any financial impact if I had given up my apartment.

To summarize the discussion about the financial impact, it is at the same time interesting and disturbing to see that all the financial impact is due to being afraid to entirely leave my comfort zone rather than it is due to taking a year off. Throughout the entire time I justified keeping my apartment by the security it offers and the fact that I did not know how long I was going to be away. Looking at it openly and frankly, however, it was rather my own lack of commitment and the fear of going all-in. My year off would not have been any less secure and creating a new base upon my return home would not have been a big deal either, but I would have spent 600 Euros less per month. Consequently, the impact on my security was only a perceived one, while the impact on my finances was real. Ultimately, the question was whether to trade freedom for security or security for freedom.

The version of me that decided to keep my apartment was my old ego before I departed to Ibiza, while my new ego after Thailand is a few insights wiser and would do a few things differently. Instead of keeping my apartment for a fake sense of security, I will give it up for a real sense of freedom, if I am going for another sabbatical in the future. A major justification for keeping it was the fact that I did not know how long I was going to be away. In retrospective, however, giving it up would have been smarter, even if I had returned home after the first six months. Another insight concerns the question whether to buy or rent property. The common belief of most people would be that renting provides us greater flexibility than buying. That was also my paradigm before my journey, while I now have a different view on it. The reason is twofold. On one hand, owning my own apartment would allow me more freedom to take decisions and would make me independent of a landlord's permission to sublet, while I am gone. On the other hand, a monthly 600 Euros for my own apartment, which nobody lives in, is still an investment and as such better than sunk costs that only benefit a landlord.

After all, I would have planned differently one year ago, if I had known what I know now. However, I have no doubts that going for this adventure was the right choice, even though it has cost me a certain amount of money. I am now more convinced than ever of what I wrote in the first lines of this chapter. Why should we live our whole life saving for our pension and leaving all the fun for later, while we can live a more fulfilled life if we spread work and fun equally over our lifetime? It is with a true belief if I am saying that there is nothing bad about spending some money on one of the greatest times of our life.

3.2 Friends & Family

When we think about the important aspects of a happy life, healthy relationships with family and friends rank remarkably high for almost everyone. To clarify it right away, I am not going to populate that family and friends do not matter. However, after my year abroad I am more convinced than ever that good relationships are not a question of location, but a question of our motivation to maintain them. It is a relevant and reasonable question if our relationships will not suffer from being abroad for one year. My first job after university was in consulting, a lifestyle that obviously requires to travel and be on the road a lot. Consequently, it was not with big surprise that my employer put efforts into establishing the mindset that friendships and relations do not depend on distance and location. Back then I could not be convinced, but now my perspective and opinion has changed.

Friendships are much more about quality than quantity. This simple idea does not only apply to how many friends we need, but also to the question what makes a good relationship, respectively how much time we need to spend with someone to call them a good friend. I have spent a great deal of my student life travelling around Europe as a member of an international student organization. Consequently, my good friends are scattered all around the globe, some of which I see every few months, but some others I have not seen for several years. Notwithstanding, my relations with some of them are much deeper and meaningful than those with some of the people back home, who I see at least once a week. Therefore, it did not have any significant impact on my network of friends, since there is no difference between keeping them alive from Ibiza or Thailand instead of my hometown. Instead, it turned out as an interesting experiment to find out which friendships really matter, and which ones are worth putting effort in, when you are away. The only difference and new challenge, when I was in Thailand, was the different time zone to my friends in Europe. However, it is a challenge to overcome much more than a problem, when we live in times of social media and emails.

It comes with great relief to realize that after being away for one year I do not have any friends less than before. Instead, I am confident to say that it is rather the opposite, since it is not a big surprise that one gets to know significantly more people travelling than living a mediocre life in one's hometown forever. It would, of course, be naïve to believe that you spend an equal amount of time with all acquaintances from your old life. There are many people wh I used to see at least once a week, who I have not spoken to for several months now. However, if losing regular contact to lose acquaintances, there will always be new ones along the way. Looking at it openly, my year abroad turned out as an interesting experiment to find out which friendships really matter. One might expect that, while I was home for 18 days after half of my sabbatical, my acquaintances and friends back home were eager to learn how Ibiza went and what I was planning for Thailand, but it came as an eye-opener that the interest was very low. After a short initial expression of appreciation for me being back, the conversations returned quickly to where I had left them six months earlier. There were almost no deeper conversations or true interest about how my adventure was going and what it meant for me.

Good and meaningful relationships will, on the other hand, remain or even grow due to becoming more interesting or coincidentally finding out about common passions. It is in this context an interesting twist in my life that during my time in Thailand I entered a love relationship with a girl, who I had been friends with for more than ten years. I am tempted to believe that this twist was not destiny or coincidence, but partly due to finding our common ambition to break loose from the 9-to-5 scheme and explore opportunities to achieve independence from any specific location. And if it was not that, it was probably due to me breaking loose from my old boring life and becoming a more interesting, resting in myself and open person. With no doubt one becomes a more attractive person, when not focusing only on getting things from their to-do list done, but rather being and living in the moment. As the reader will find out later, it was a major outcome for me to shift my focus from doing to being.

Finally, my relationship with my family improved a lot, while I lived abroad. It does not come as a big surprise, when considering that parental main interest is likely to be that their children live a happy and fulfilled life. As such, I had already expected before leaving and was confirmed while abroad that family will always hold on to you anyways, no matter where in the world you are and what it takes. The most significant impact on this relationship, however, was that our conversations became much deeper and more meaningful, as there were many more experiences and challenges to share.

To summarize, I am confident to say that living one of the greatest adventures of my life until this point has not had any negative impact on my relationships with family and friends. Instead, it has been an interesting insight which friendships really matter, and I have gotten to know a lot of new people, while my relationship with my family improved and a new love relationship began. After all, many of the people I got to know in Ibiza and Thailand turned out as meaningful as my acquaintances at home but sharing a greater sense of common passion. So, if someone now asks me how being away for one year influenced my social environment, I can with sincere confidence say that it foremostly made me feel like a stranger at home and made me more convinced than ever that real friendships have nothing to do with location, but rather with having a genuine interest into each other.

3.3 Career

There is one aspect of life, which on a first sight one year of diving does not go well along with. Most of us have some professional career, which we follow through our life, some of us with more ambitious career goals than others. When I shared my plans to take a break and go diving for one year, I faced a lot of scepticism. The reactions ranged from "But how does that fit into a corporate career?" from one of my friends to "You will never make it back into a normal work life!" from my line manager, when I informed him about my resignation. It would be naïve to say that these feedbacks did not make me doubt, but fortunately enough none of these prophecies became true in the end. It was quite the opposite instead. As I will explain a few lines further down this chapter, it came as a big surprise what happened a few weeks after my departure to Ibiza, a surprise that made my re-entry into the corporate world much easier than expected.

Before we go in more detail into the events from June 2019 onwards, we shall have a brief discussion about the meaning of work itself. Without having conducted a survey to prove this hypothesis, it is easy to suspect that most people will express that earning the money to pay our bills is the first and foremost, if not even the only, meaning of work. However, when we think about it from a wider perspective, we realize that our monthly salary is only a very superficial benefit of work. It would be wrong to deny that we need to work to pay our bills, but there is way more that work can do for us.

If we have a job, which we are passionate about, we do not even need money to motivate us to get up in the morning. It will be the result of the work itself that keeps us going. When designed in the right manner, enabling employees to see it through to the end, work can give us a purpose, the essence that makes us want to move forward. If it furthermore also involves the right level of challenge, one that neither exceeds our ability to learn nor bores us, our daily tasks can and will contribute to our growth. The growth potential is not even limited to learning new skills and capabilities required to get our work done, but it can also grow us as humans making us more mature and enriching our attitude and perspective on many areas of life.

The reality of modern work is, unfortunately, quite different. Many of us spend their days waiting for the moment they can go home, their week waiting for

Friday and their year waiting for the next vacation. Work has become the main source of frustration and despair for many people, which is very saddening when we consider how big a part of our life we spend at the workplace. We are so caught up and trapped in the daily rat race, trying to not drown in the increasing number of demands placed upon us, that we cannot spare the time to think about the meaning of our work and forget that after all we are meant to live a life that fulfils us. We get home after nine or ten hours in the office, leaving behind more new tasks than completed ones, and will often continue thinking about work in our free time. Many people get so much of their energy, motivation and spirit drained by their hated jobs that depression, burnout, anxiety and loss of joy have become very common phenomena these days.

When I am now looking back to the early days of 2019, it hurts to realize how close to burnout I was. I was not there yet and did not even realize, as I was too busy working through my daily to-do lists. Now that I gained some distance from my old life and started to rest in myself, however, it is disturbing to realize my state of mind one year ago. Fortunately, I managed to jump of the treadmill before it was too late. So, to which extent did my year off ruin my career, as my line manager predicted?

Because I had come to hate my old job a lot, it comes with no surprise that over the last couple of months before I finally resigned, I had placed a significant number of applications at various companies. It was the successful completion of my Instructor Training Course that made me stop applying, as it enabled me to achieve my long-held dream before finding myself a new workplace. As I wrote earlier in this book, it was on purpose that I went to Ibiza without knowing what comes after. Having been caught in the hamster wheel of a work, which solely served to pay my bills and to cover the flaws of a mediocre life with monetary means, a major hope for my time outside the rat race was to gain insight and clarity on my passions, so that I could find a job that fits into them.

It was less than a month after I moved to Ibiza, when a friend of mine working for a company, which I had unsuccessfully applied to twice, asked for my permission to share my contact data with their Human Resources department again. Having learnt about my resignation from my old job they had become interested in new discussions about the possibility to employ me. While I was at first very sceptical, as I did not want to commit to anything yet, I did not want to shut this door either. So it happened that I had a first phone interview from the beach of Ibiza, a personal meeting when I was home between Ibiza and Thailand and, finally, a ready to be signed work contract in my hands before I even left to the second leg of my journey. It still took me a few weeks to feel comfortable to sign this contract, but at the beginning of 2020 I had found myself a job for my return to Germany. I will discuss further down in this book what made me hesitate to sign the contract and how I got ready in the end.

There are three eye-opening and mind-changing facts in how I came to this new job. Firstly, it still strikes me a lot that I got a new highly paid full-time and permanent job without having placed a single application. It feels a bit like a victory to prove my previous line manager wrong with his prophecy that I will ruin my entire career and struggle to get back into the corporate world. Secondly, it becomes even more striking when I consider my new employer's feedback that they had become explicitly interested to talk again when learning about my resignation and my decision to go abroad. It even seems to be a general trend these days that these side-tracks in our CVs make us more interesting for employers, as they make us stand out from the huge number of applications as well as they prove us to be proactive and entrepreneurial to some degree. When looking back, I can conclude and am convinced that this adventure of mine has grown in me some of the characteristics which can be found in many job postings. Thirdly and lastly, I received another interesting feedback during my interviews. It is no surprise that at some point I had to answer the question how long I planned to stay abroad, respectively by when I would be available for my new job. All I could say at that point was that I did not know yet. I was convinced that this would ruin everything and mark the end of our conversation. Their reaction was, surprisingly and fortunately, a different one, as they told me that I should enjoy my time in Thailand, and we would find a date when I was ready. The logic was simple. It is more in an employer's interest to wait a bit longer and get someone sustainably rather than having to start the recruiting process again sooner or later.

To summarize these three interesting facts, I can conclude that going off the common track for one year has in no way ruined my career. There is always a way back and it turned out much easier than I anticipated. All I lost was some income that I did, however, not need anymore, since scuba diving and travelling as my previous main expenditures had now become my life and profession. It is only important to avoid turning prophecies, as the one from my previous line manager, into self-fulfilling ones. It is way too easy to become our own greatest obstacles, if we place to much focus and belief onto anything, which others want to make us believe. If we, however, give in to these societal prophecies, we revert to following that external script, which has been embedded in our thinking way too deep, and hold ourselves back from living the life we want. Being the only species on earth with self-awareness, it is our ultimate responsibility to understand our most inner desires and live a life that serves them. We need to take the feedback and thoughts of the people around us as what they are. We shall not decline that they are a healthy source of second thought and inspiration, but we must not sacrifice our own will to prophecies of people, who know our ambitions less than we do.

While it should by now be clear that working as scuba diving instructor for one year has in no way ruined my career, the question remains in how far I see this experience enrich my career and life. I had to face the question and, to be honest, needed some time to come to terms with it, how I could justify spending seven years at university and then not staying within that profession. When we, however, look at all the various impacts of nowadays digitalization, globalization, and other contemporary trends, we face an endless variety of opportunities how we can earn money and live our life. Would it then not be a shame if we spend our entire life in the same work and place instead of discovering what else the world has to offer? While the mindset and lifestyle of our parents' generation was a different one and staying in the same job until retirement was normal, paradigms have changed and it is becoming increasingly common and normal that people built up diverse CVs and explore different paths of life.

Once I had come to terms with letting my university education be what it was, an episode and limited period of my life, I had freed my mind and enabled all the positive impacts of following an uncontroversial path to reach into my consciousness. While my job in Ibiza was even more stressful than my previous life, since I moved up to working six days a week, I started to rest way more in myself, as my work started to tap into my passion. Working on something, which I was passionate about, resulted in two impressive changes of mind. Firstly, I had always been counting down the days to the weekend in my old office job, while the weekdays did not matter at all in Thailand. Consequently, I hardly ever knew what day of the week it was. Even now that I am writing these lines from a café in Saigon, it takes me a moment to remember that it is Friday. I have come to live in the moment. Secondly, money has become a side effect of work much more than the only motivation. Before I left for Ibiza, I did not have to worry about money at all but was nevertheless always waiting for the next pay check at the end of the month. This changed entirely from May 2019. While I was by far not as financially secure as before anymore, it was not money that motivated me to do my job. It was meeting interesting people, inspiring them for a new hobby and growing myself as an instructor and human that motivated me to get out of bed in the morning. I had found a purpose in my work.

Reflecting on how these months in Ibiza and Thailand have grown me as a person and considering the previously discussed feedback from my new employer, I am more convinced than ever that my sabbatical has enriched my professional attitude and will support my professional progression in the long-term. It is a common understanding these days that such side-tracks in our CVs are an advantage when applying for a job. If it is not only for standing out from the high number of applications, which need to pass through the pre-selection by Human Resource departments, they are also evidence of characteristics sought by employers in their candidates. After all, thinking outside the box and a proven ability to find solutions for uncommon challenges are some of the requirements that can be read in many vacancies, as they can make the difference between an average and a high performer.

Ultimately, these traits are often also considered important for successful entrepreneurs. While I was far from being an entrepreneur, before I embarked to Thailand, I returned with a significantly greater entrepreneurial spirit. My focus shifted from spending 40 hours per week in an office doing what pleased my boss to accepting unlimited responsibility for my own success, building and maintaining helpful networks and doing whatever it takes to be successful. While I had a variety of stakeholders keeping me busy before Thailand, I now suddenly had to become my own driving force. As a freelancer it was ultimately my very own responsibility to keep myself busy, while the other alternative was to use the off-season as excuse to enjoy the beach life of Thailand. Thus, I am convinced that the experiences, which I made as scuba diving instructor, will support my professional progression in the long-term, while that has not even been my goal when I decided to take this journey.

When I departed from Germany at the beginning of 2019, it felt as if I was jumping off the treadmill that my job and life had become. The need to pay for my life was the only reason that kept me going to my office five days a week, a life which I spent dreaming of that day in the future when I would finally be a scuba diving instructor and break loose. I was at that point, however, denying the fact that I would at some point have to answer myself the question what would come afterwards. Experiencing for one year how it feels when your work connects to your passion and what it means to accept unlimited responsibility for your success as a freelancer has been an immensely powerful lesson. As will be discussed in greater depth further down in this book, I am now more convinced than ever what I expect from my career respectively what I do not. If I will now be strong enough to go that way, my one year as a scuba diving instructor will not only enrich my future career but also my future life in general. This experience has become the trim tab I hoped for and grown in me a vision for the future.

Before I move on to discuss one more common belief that makes people stuck in a mediocre life, I can now answer some questions I raised a bit earlier. It is for me not a philosophical question anymore if we are meant to spend our life making a career that makes us unhappy or living a happy and fulfilled life. I have now answered for myself the question if I want to live to work or work to life. The answer for me is that this is not even a question, when you do something you like, as the boundaries between work and life disappear and it all becomes just a great deal of fun.

3.4 Being Afraid to Fail

Even if we reduce our fixed costs to set up our financial base for a year abroad and are neither afraid of ruining our career nor losing any friends, we must still avoid or overcome one common mindset. The fear of failing prevents us way too often from growth opportunities and, consequently, holds us back from living a fulfilled life. It does not come with big surprise how big a leap out of my comfort zone it was to inform my company about my resignation and board a flight to Ibiza without having booked a return ticket yet. The leap out of the by then expanded comfort zone, when I decided to go to Thailand without having a work contract fixed, was obviously even bigger. I am now, however, happy that I took these steps, as it is outside our comfort zones where life awaits, and growth happens.

Being afraid to fail will prevent us from many of the good things in life. It starts with the seemingly small things such as making new friends, when you move to a new place, or approaching someone you find attractive, when you are tired of living your life as a single. What may seem a small thing and regular part of life for the more self-confident ones among us, can turn into a big obstacle for the ones, who are afraid of rejections. When thinking about the possible outcome objectively, though, even a "no" will not leave us worse off than if we had not tried. The same applies to the bigger decisions in life. Much can go different than planned when taking major decisions, such as quitting your job to work as a scuba diving instructor for one year. After all, if I had allowed these doubts and fear of failure to prevent me from going this step, I would now not be sitting on the beach of Koh Tao writing this book. I would instead be doing the same disliked job as before, living the same mediocre and unfulfilling life. I would be filled with regret that I am not living the life I want to live. What these two examples from entirely different areas of life have in common is the fact that we need to be ready to fail or we will get stuck and not move on in life.

A common saying says that you can fail when you try, but you already failed if you do not try. The safest way to avoid failing or losing our face is to do the very same things, which we master in perfection, repeatedly. While this may seem like a desirable way to achieve routine and comfort, it will with an equal degree of certainty prevent us from acquiring new skills, learning new hobbies, and moving on in life. Even if we do not remember in all detail, it has most certainly taken us a great deal of frustration to learn to walk as a child and, later in life, a lot of frustrating feedback from our instructor, when we were getting prepared for our driver's license exam. Fortunately, as a young child we have not yet been socially conditioned to be afraid of losing our face. We try to walk, just to fall and get up to try again as often as it takes. When we now imagine how different our life would look, if fear of failure had prevented us from learning these essential skills, the importance of our willingness to leave our comfort zone becomes clear. One might now argue that learning to walk can hardly be compared to working as a scuba diving instructor for one year. I agree that there is a significant difference as such that one is an essential life skill, while the other is a bonus on top of an already well-established life. However, the underlying paradigm applies to both. The more we are ready to take steps out of our comfort zone and risk to fail, the more fun, excitement, satisfaction and growth we will achieve in our life.

During my university time I had taken several significant steps out of my comfort zone, as I lived in Australia for eight months as an exchange student, applied and got elected for the international board of an international student organization and moved to a different part of Germany for a six-months internship. All these decisions have scared me a lot at their time and each of these periods has come with many challenges and has not always been easy. However, each of them has rewarded me with a lot of growth and I am able to pinpoint specifically which major and important developments each of them has triggered in me. All these steps out of my comfort zone have paid off and I would be less mature if I had given in to the fear of failure.

An entirely different period in life began soon after my graduation. After one year in consulting I felt a dire desire for routine and establishment. Getting myself a 9-to-5 job in my hometown provided exactly this. An increased routine and stability, however, came with reduced excitement and growth and after a while a dire desire to break loose again. Reflecting on my time in Ibiza and Thailand leads me to another interesting insight. Whereas the first three abovementioned periods of my life, each of them relatively short in time, have created memories lasting for a lifetime, the seven years following graduation merely passed by. I had gotten stuck in my comfort zone and had created myself a mediocre life. Fortunately, my frustration about the mediocracy of my life reached the necessary level for me to be ready to step out. The pain had exceeded my fear. It comes with great satisfaction to realize that my one year abroad has created new lasting memories, which will nurture me for a long time, and triggered a lot of growth, as will be discussed in more detail in the next chapter.

As comes with no surprise, I was as nervous and scared at the beginning of 2019, when my departure to Ibiza was approaching, as I was in November 2019, when I was home after Ibiza getting ready for my departure to Thailand. Even though my six months in Ibiza had already been a big step, the leap out of my comfort zone was still bigger when going to Thailand. When taking the decision for Ibiza at the end of 2018, it was one of the other options to go to Koh Tao right away. Looking back in all honesty now, my decision to go to Ibiza was due to my fear of taking my second leg out of the comfort zone much more than there were actual advantages of Ibiza over Koh Tao. It comes with some regret that I did not go the big step right away, but fortunately my decision to go to Koh Tao in November proves one interesting fact about comfort zones. No matter how big the step out of them is, we will start feeling comfortable again as the comfort zone grows, making us ready for bigger steps. Every step leaves us a bigger and stronger person than before. While the move to Koh Tao scared me too much at the beginning of 2019, I did not fear that step as much anymore by late summer of the same year.

As discussed before, my journey scared me a lot, fear of failure playing an important role in it. If I now had the wrong mindset and focus when looking at the last year, I would even fall into the trap to consider it a failure. After all, Ibiza did neither provide the glorious lifestyle I envisioned, nor did I teach the courses I wanted to teach. Later I did not teach as many students on Koh Tao as I envisioned, consequently not being able to make this period financially sustainable. It would be entirely wrong, though, to take these downsides as reasons to consider my journey a failure. In the end, I did have a good time, learnt a lot about myself and grew a lot not only as a scuba diving instructor but also as a person, a growth that would not have been possible if I had resigned to the fear of failure. Consequently, my year abroad was a success, as I achieved what I wanted to achieve. The downsides listed above are what they are, but it would anyways be naïve to assume that one year will not come with any negative aspects. Ultimately, it is our own choice to focus our awareness on the positive aspects, while we take the negative ones as the growth and development opportunities they are. If we, however, avoid stepping into the unknown, there may appear to be many successes to celebrate. However, each of them comes with the great cost of a greater success we missed.

While my year abroad leaves me with a drastically expanded comfort zone, which will make significant decisions and steps in the future a lot easier, I would find myself more trapped than ever in a vicious cycle down the path of regret, if I had returned after Ibiza or not taken this journey at all. Regret is a strong and powerful obstacle on the way out of mediocracy and towards success. Having a dream without realizing it will keep it on our thoughts, making it hard if not impossible to focus our mind elsewhere and give the best we can in our work, relationships and life in general. Our life will become even more unsuccessful, we will blame ourselves and regret will grow even stronger until we reach a decision point of no return. Then it is up to us to take the decision which path we want to follow, either the mediocre path of resigning from our dreams and ambitions or the proactive path of working up the courage to break out of our socially conditioned pattern and live the life we desire.

I have taken that decision a while ago and, while it scared me at first, I am now happy that I took the proactive path. If I had not gone to Koh Tao after Ibiza, I would have returned home full of regret that I had only gone half-heartedly instead of doing what I really wanted to do. At the end of my time in Koh Tao I achieved peace of mind and felt ready to return home to start the next leg of my life, while a strong desire to break free again would have remained if I had gone home by the end of 2019. Even more, returning after Ibiza would have caused a high chance of going back into my old life and missing a great opportunity to break free, while I now feel ready to start a new life and use my sabbatical as a trim tab towards something better.

After all, even if for whatever reason this adventure had turned out as a failure entirely, it would not have left me broke and ruined. There is always a way back, if we manage to jump off early enough, and all that remains after some time are life experiences and, ultimately, interesting stories to tell. In the end, it is the unsuccessful and challenging periods of our life that grow us and leave us stronger much more than the easy and mediocre phases of life can do.

Having discussed how leaving the comfort zone and being ready to fail will lead to great achievements, it is now time to elaborate more specifically what my gap year has triggered in me and how it has grown me as a person. When I am now reflecting on my life until May 2019 and the months that followed, I can identify two main driving forces, which triggered several important and valuable developments in me.

Firstly, my income reduced drastically, and I could only fit a limited number of belongings into my suitcase. While it is a common belief that money cannot buy you happiness, I am now even going one step further. After living a simple life for twelve months the experience has proven to me that money can rather be a significant contributor to being unhappy. As I do not want to offend any of the poorer ones among us, I acknowledge that a lack of funds leads to many problems and does not make us happy either. I have experienced that myself while spending several years at university. However, giving up a well-paid job after several years now made me realize how I had used purchases, consume and possessions to distract me from flaws and frustration in my life. It is way too easy to buy us a fake sense of satisfaction instead of identifying and working on the root cause of our frustration, even more so since the latter requires a great deal of honesty with ourselves. Thus, it was challenging at first but then came as a long-needed eye-opener to make my life lean and not be able anymore to hide my problems under unnecessary consume. Many of my developments during my eleven months away would likely not have happened if I had kept the income and wealth of the years before. After all, I traded financial wealth for spiritual and mental wealth, without even consciously doing so.

Secondly, having achieved my long-held dream of becoming a scuba diving instructor turned into a deep psychological challenge, one that I did not anticipate at all. Suddenly I found myself without a goal to work towards to, having accomplished the one that had given me a purpose for several years. While it felt on one hand great to accomplish one of my biggest dreams, it came with an intriguing insight how I had spent my last years. Looking back in honesty now, I had gotten used to living a somewhat mediocre life in my own little bubble, using my future as an excuse for not making the changes that were necessary. It was psychologically significantly easier to believe that happiness will find me automatically, once I become a scuba diving instructor, than to take an honest look at the flaws in my life, accept full and unlimited responsibility and, ultimately, put myself into the driver's seat of my life. The sudden absence of a goal together with the dire realization that happiness will not find me automatically, even if I am living the life of the people, I had been admiring for years, made it impossible to let the future any longer keep me from living my life now.

As my most important excuse was gone, I was no longer able to ignore many of the things in my life, which I had closed my eyes from for too long. In the end, the initial absence respectively later availability of a new goal made the difference between the need to continue to Koh Tao after Ibiza and the readiness to return home at the beginning of 2020, as the reader will learn more about later in this book.

Expectedly, leaving my comfort zone and bubble did not leave me unchanged. As I had been living in my comfort zone way too long, excusing the mediocracy of my life with the better future life as a scuba diving instructor, the journey, which has become the backbone of this book, had become overdue to trigger an honest look at my life and make the changes that were necessary. No longer able to cover flaws with consume and excuse myself with the future, I suddenly had to accept unlimited responsibility for my life and I realized the following areas, which I had to work on.

Interestingly, the insights and developments were much deeper during my time in Thailand than the first six months of my journey. Looking at how I spent each of these periods it is not a surprise though. As I was constantly busy in Ibiza, my reflections remained relatively shallow, being rather practical changes necessary in attitude and behaviour. Since in Thailand, however, the distance to my previous life was even greater and I had more free time to spend with my own thoughts, the reflections consequently became much deeper and more meaningful. Together with the fact that as a freelancer I had to be proactive versus being externally driven to some degree in Ibiza as well as having the months in Ibiza to digest, the focus during my time in Koh Tao turned from rather practical insights towards deeper thoughts about my future. I had become ready to think about and come up with new plans and goals as well as a new vision, which was necessary after my previous goal was not there anymore.

4.1 Make Your Life Lean to Make it Complex

When I am looking back to how my life changed, when I left Germany, I realize one significant impact that may not seem pleasant at first. It is not a big surprise though that I gave up a high degree of security, structure and routine and traded it for uncertainty, complications and needs to organize and improvise. Some people might now wonder why one would voluntarily give up the security of a well-established life and unnecessarily complicate everything. While I am admittedly also having these thoughts in some of my weaker moments, the answer is easy though. It is routine and structure that easily leads us into a mediocre life, while an exciting, memorable and meaningful life is closely linked to complications and challenging moments to overcome. As such I did not only give up security, structure and routine, but I also gave up mediocracy and unhappiness trading it for satisfaction.

It comes convenient to trigger further thoughts for this book that I am writing these lines during March 2020. I am scheduled to return to Europe in twelve days, while the world is facing what is likely to turn out as the greatest challenge of the century. Europe has recently been declared the epicentre of the global COVID-19 pandemic. European countries are closing their borders and suspending air travel to many destinations. Visa regulations worldwide are made stricter and among others, people from Germany are banned from entering many countries worldwide. The next containment measures are as difficult to foresee as how long it will take to get back to a normal state. I am far from calling these developments positive or exciting and they do certainly not contribute to my happiness, but they signify what is important in how we approach the complications and challenges of our life. It is easy to lose our spirit in challenging times, but if we stand strong and approach them thoughtfully and mindfully, we will learn from them and leave them stronger than before. After all, even this new pandemic will probably be under control at some point and become one temporary episode in our life, a hopefully relatively short one in relation to our entire life.

We need to make our life lean in materialistic terms to enable us to enrich it spiritually. When I moved to Ibiza,

I left most of my belongings behind and drastically cut my expenses, as discussed in the previous chapter. In fact, I did not take much more luggage than I would take on a regular vacation and, as I experienced throughout the months to follow, I did not miss anything. While I lived in a decent apartment and watched television almost every night in Germany, I lived with basic conditions in Ibiza and have by now been watching almost no television for one year. In fact, I had to realize that I still took way too many belongings with me to Ibiza. Many of the clothes or other things remained unused and the first time I touched them was after six months, when I packed my luggage for my trip back to Germany. As a result, I decided to take between 15 and 20 kg less with me to Thailand and still I am not missing anything. Even after this further reduction of my luggage there were certain pieces that remained unused until I left Koh Tao.

While the need to make my life lean came as an important insight itself, it was also making my life lean that triggered many of the further insights which I will discuss. Having freed myself from the materialistic ballast of my old life and having eliminated the distractions called possessions, which enabled me to keep my eyes closed from the flaws in my life, I had suddenly freed my mind to recognize what the crucial ingredients of a fulfilled life are. It was to a big degree the cut in my belongings that made me realize many of the things I need to work on, as they will be discussed throughout this chapter. Living a simple life in simple accommodation placed the focus on positive thoughts, a meaningful purpose, healthy relationships and a time well spent as opposed to income, consume and possession which had been the focus of my life way too long. A complete life does certainly not depend on materialistic things and we certainly do not need much to live a complete life. It is no surprise that this reflection was not easy to accept, as all meaningful and life-changing insights come with pain and regret of some degree. I am, however, convinced that it will contribute significantly to my future happiness.

It has today become a widely believed theory that materialistic and monetary benefits only motivate and drive us if we do not have them. Once they become a minor concern for us, they lose their motivating power. It is interesting to see how this theory was proven during my time in Ibiza and Koh Tao. By the time I boarded my flight to Ibiza I had spent seven years in a well-paid job and left with a significant extraordinary pay-check for the overtime, which I had accrued in the last year and could not get rid of before I left. As a result, I did in Ibiza never care about any monetary aspects of my work and did instead get all my motivation from the individual challenges of each student and the joy of meeting new exciting people with every course I started. And it felt great. Unfortunately, my source of motivation started shifting during my time in Koh Tao, when my financial situation was nearing the point that

I would have to touch my long-term savings. Even though I knew that using some of them would be worth it and not ruin me, this fact started to enter my awareness with an irresistible power. The relief came when I had a fixed date for my return to Germany. At least I thought that I had a fixed date, as my return turned out more difficult than I thought, as I will elaborate at the end of this chapter. However, as the mathematics whether my funds would last long enough became easier by having a date, I started to rest in myself significantly more and became more comfortable only doing those courses that promised a sense of achievement and to take me forward as an instructor. As SSI grants experience and recognition levels to their professionals based on the number of certifications we issue, I noticed that I started to be significantly more motivated by courses leading to actual certifications than basic acquisition programs. Money had partially lost its motivating potential again. And it felt great again!

One might now wonder if these thoughts are not contrary to what I wrote a bit earlier about making our life lean in materialistic terms. It can appear as a logical conclusion that eliminating some of our belongings will weaken our financial safety net and, therefore, shift our focus away from purpose towards money as a motivating factor. However, possessions and belongings are no capital that we can easily spend, as it is tied up capital and can, furthermore, lead to additional costs. The simple presence of all the furniture, books and other things in my apartment played a significant role in my decision to not give up my apartment in Germany, a decision that made my financial situation during my year off a lot tighter. I now have learnt from my own experience that materialistic assets may provide us a false sense of security but do in fact rather create a not negligible obstacle holding us back from living our life to the fullest. Thus, we need to make our life lean in materialistic terms, not only to enrich it spiritually but also to give us more flexibility for change.

As I have already elaborated, my life before Ibiza contained a high level of structure, routine and predictability but, consequently, a low level of excitement and satisfaction. The fear of failure and leaving my comfort zone had been holding me back for several years. In contrast, as soon as I moved to Koh Tao, my life became complex with a big degree of uncertainty and need to organize things, for which I did have no clue how they work in Thailand. It did, expectedly, not take long until I first started doubting if it could not have saved me a lot of hassles to stay home. However, as we have discussed in detail already, we need to take on these challenges if we want to grow as humans and move forward in our life. I am now happy that I accepted these challenges, as I would have otherwise missed a great life-changing experience. Furthermore, I am convinced that it has grown me a lot to solve these challenges and that the experience will make any future challenges appear smaller and easier to solve, consequently opening doors for new and bigger adventures. As already discussed, doing the same thing repetitively and not changing your routines will bring the least challenges and the greatest security, but also the least excitement and satisfaction.

There was one habit I had to change to make the organization of my life easier and to accept the complications that came along. Having worked as a project manager for several years, I was used to organizing every day of my life, which for me included printing out important information and putting it on my desk in a chronological order. I was used to printing out every flight ticket and every email, which contained information potentially useful during a trip. As soon as something was not well organized with contingency plans in place, I got nervous and felt restless. This, however, is not only impractical when you are out travelling and for example book your flights through your phone, but it also gets time consuming when you need to find a print shop for every page you want to print. Thus, I had to make two changes to not get lost in the increased complexity of my life abroad.

On one hand, it required a change in mindset and paradigms. I had to learn to let go and to feel at ease even though not everything was organized and there were no contingency plans for everything that could potentially go wrong. In other words, I had to trust my ability to handle challenges when they arise to spend my time enjoying my life instead of only organizing it. This was also an interesting learning opportunity, not only in the sense that I realized I can trust this ability of mine but also in the sense that I further improved myself and will be better able to organize life and deal with unexpected issues in the future, helping me to keep my life lean and rest more in myself. On the other hand, I needed to move my organization digital. There is nowadays no need to bring a printed ticket to the airport, when everything you need is contained in an email. There is not even a need for an internet connection, as emails are commonly available offline once synchronized and for the rest it just takes some organization to download the necessary files onto your phone, whenever there is internet at the airports, cafes or similar places. After all, making my organization lean by moving it digital enabled me to make my life itself more complex and, consequently, more meaningful and satisfactory.

Once we accept the advantages of a lean life, it does not take long to realize that a leaner life furthermore leads to a decreased fear of failing. As it should be clear by now, possessions and belongings do not provide any safety net, but do instead hold us back, as they make significant decisions and moves in life more difficult and a big barrier to overcome. After all, no matter how great your adventure is, there is always a way back, if we identify a sensible point by when to jump off the adventure. I had set as a limit for myself that I did not want to touch my long-term savings, a limit which seems wise with an increasing degree by the time I am writing these lines.

At the time, when I typed the opening lines for this chapter, in the early days of March 2020, I was happily teaching and living in Koh Tao, nevertheless looking forward to my flight to Germany on March 26th, as it implied seeing my girlfriend again the day after. I was still living life in paradise, partially denying what was happening in the rest of the world, while life in the rest of the world went on as usual despite first indications that this would change soon. By the time I am writing these lines now on 18th March 2020 Europe has seen two weeks of developments nobody could have imagined a few weeks ago. The European Union has closed its borders for the rest of the world, attempting to encourage member states to re-open internal borders. Several airlines have grounded their planes and ceased their operations, not being the only business that is hit by the fact that global economy is nearing recession. Entire countries are on shutdown, police enforcing people to stay at home in democratic western countries, where this has never seemed possible. COVID-19 has brought life to a stillstand as it has never been seen before. As I am now writing these lines from Stockholm, the current pandemic and crisis makes me reflect on my journey in several ways.

First and foremost, as it relates to "Make Your Life Lean to Make it Complex", it has torn my entire planning apart. Until 14th March 2020 my plan was to go on a four-nights diving liveaboard in the Similan Islands, as a last great time before my return flight would take me home on 26th March 2020. It was on 14th March 2020, however, when this flight was cancelled with no re-booking offered and it became obvious that no next containment measures in Germany and the rest of Europe were impossible. Therefore, I found myself sitting down on 15th March booking a flight to Stockholm for 16th March to get there before further borders closed and I would not be able to see my girlfriend for a while, probably the shortest notice ever by which I booked a long-distance flight.

As I now had to get ready for departure in less than 24 hours, including selling my motorbike, moving out of my apartment and packing my luggage, while not forgetting to bid goodbye to the people on Koh Tao, I could prove to myself my ability to solve challenges as they arise, while I had no time to overly organize or unnecessarily print documents. I learnt to acknowledge the possibility to keep the organization of my life lean while I experienced the benefits of it in the most powerful way. However, it was not only readiness to keep my organization lean, which shortened my reaction time to a degree necessary to leave Koh Tao on such a short notice, but also the fact that I had by then learned to keep my life lean in materialistic terms. Over the last years I travelled a lot and have, consequently, developed a routine that lets me pack my luggage in almost no time. However, this time I was leaving four months of life behind and was relocating instead of going for vacation. Nevertheless, packing my luggage took less than an hour despite having my complete set of diving gear with me, an advantage of having only few belongings with me. One might imagine now the impossibility of leaving within 24 hours, if I had to ship parts of my belongings as parcel.

In addition, this experience has proven the rationale behind defining a reasonable exit point. As elaborated before, I had set for myself as a limit to not consume my long-term savings. It turned out as a wise decision in the light of these unforeseen developments, as my savings in their form of stock market investments were devaluing drastically, while it became increasingly difficult to anticipate economic impacts such as development of the job market or my ability to start my new job on 1st May. However, there were also more direct and immediate impacts as for instance the cost associated with booking my flight home on such a short notice. Since my financial buffer at this point was still big enough, partly due to having cleaned up my finances and having gotten rid of unnecessary costs, these developments did of course bother to a certain degree, but not ruin my further plans.

Looking back at my entire journey now I am happy that I have made my life lean in three regards. Already when I moved to Ibiza but even more when I moved to Koh Tao, I kept my life lean in materialistic terms. The result was an enriched spiritual life in the sense of shifting my focus to what really matters, alongside an impressively short reaction time in the light of unforeseen developments. Further, I eliminated unnecessary fixed costs, which resulted in higher financial flexibility and more remaining financial buffer when it was needed towards the end of my journey. It was impressive how many unnecessary costs I had accumulated over time. Lastly, it was that I kept my organization lean and moved it digital, which not only allowed me to add as much fun into my life as I did but also contributed to the short reaction time during my last days in Thailand, without which it would have been difficult to leave Koh Tao in less than 24 hours.

It was this elimination of dependencies in my life that decreased my fear of failure and expanded my comfort zone. Consequently, it set the base for making my life more complex and enriching it in many ways. While I had high security, little challenge and a lot of mediocracy in my life before Ibiza, my happiness increased with each of the two legs of my journey, as security decreased and the number of challenges increased. Ultimately, it was this readiness to make my life lean which enabled me to leave mediocracy behind and live an exciting year full of fulfilment. I am, therefore, happy that I made my life lean, in order to make it complex.

4.2 Spend Your Life Being Instead of Doing

By the time I moved to Ibiza I had been working in project management for six years, a job that typically goes along with spending most of your time developing action plans, drawing schedules and controlling progress. It is probably healthy to develop habits for our private life, which are contrary to how we are spending our professional life, while it is not unlikely that the way we spend these 40 whatsoever hours a week will not leave us unchanged. Apparently, it did not work out well for me, however, as I now realize more than ever that I had adopted a significant portion of my work habits also for the rest of my life.

I am now struggling to identify exactly how far ago I have developed that paradigm leading to an unhealthy habit which has stuck with me until today. It appears, however, that it was already during my university time that I started seeing life not as the goal itself but as the means to achieve something yet to be defined. I started feeling uncomfortable, whenever I spent my time on something that was according to my own understanding an unproductive use of time. Unfortunately, this mentality grew even stronger throughout the years following graduation. By the time I left for Ibiza my self-imposed to-do lists had gained a big degree of control over my life. I spent my entire life doing instead of being. It is, of course, on one hand a mindset that promises to spend your time effectively, getting a lot done. It is on the other hand, however, also a paradigm that prevents us from being in the moment and living a happy life.

I cannot and do not want to deny that the use of some self-management tools contributes to structure in our life and is, therefore, a powerful support in achieving our goals and dreams. I have always been and am still convinced that it is important to have dreams and goals for our life and that we must work towards them in a structured manner. These two beliefs had, however, gone out of control and my sabbatical was overdue to set my mentality right again.

We must never sacrifice being human and living in the moment for the sake of spending our time productively. This is, however, exactly what I had gotten used to by the beginning of 2019. I was no longer using my to-do list as a tool to free my mind and steer my priorities but instead it controlled a big portion of my thinking. No matter how effectively I was working on something of high meaning and importance, the unattended needs for action, no matter how small and meaningless they were, kept on distracting me from what really matters. Instead of spending my time mindfully and feeling good about what I was doing I had developed a deep habit of regretting the things I was not doing. Even pleasant things, such as hobbies and dinners with friends, had become boxes to tick off. Instead of mindfully enjoying those pleasant moments and going with the flow my thoughts were usually with the next things on my agenda. In the evenings I always reflected upon how productive my day had been but never on how I had felt and how well I had rested in myself. In other words, I always reflected on how I had done but never on how I had been. Recognizing moments of being instead of doing led to regret due to feeling unproductive, while I should have appreciated those moments as what life is about.

As I wrote a bit earlier, I am still convinced that it is important to have meaningful goals and dreams for our life. In fact, as I already indicated and will discuss in more detail later in this book, it was the appearance of a new goal that made me ready to return home from Koh Tao. While it is important to work towards our goals, we must not sacrifice living our life. Instead, we must see our goals as what they are, a direction and guiding force. Life must not only be seen as a means towards a certain achievement, but also a meaning itself. We must never sacrifice being for the sake of doing. After all, I am not only writing this book to have it published at some point. It is equally important to me to work on it to digest the experiences, which I am making during these twelve months.

It turned out that a few specific changes in my environment and lifestyle triggered a healthy change in my mindset during my time in Ibiza and, even stronger, during my time in Koh Tao. While it was at first highly challenging for me as an introvert person to be suddenly surrounded by people all the time and live with almost no privacy in Ibiza, it turned out extremely healthy to accept that challenge and have people questioning what I was doing, if I was not spending my time with them. After having lived a big portion of my life on my own, I was now getting inspired and challenged a lot by the people around me and it confirmed that these two are highly crucial benefits of healthy relationships.

It, furthermore, turned out as a significant psychological trigger to leave my old life behind for a while and start a new one. The change itself provided a great possibility to clean up mentally, as I had cumulated a lot of commitments over the last few years, many of which were not even providing purpose to me anymore. As they had become so deeply embedded in my habits, however, it required to break with my life to also break with some of these commitments. A new beginning in a new location with different people around me made it much more acceptable for my own conscience to step back and let go of some of my perceived responsibilities. Seeing a connection between my work and passion together with a sense of having arrived, where I had been wanting to be for a long time, certainly was another significant contributor in letting go of my unhealthy habit to have my life controlled by tasks and to-do lists.

The changes in my circumstances and environment provided the desperately needed trigger to start living my life more mindfully and shift my focus from only doing to being. While I sometimes still catch myself focused a lot on what my mind tells me that I must do, I feel that the last year has started a strong development into the right direction. I cannot even imagine writing this book, before I embarked on this cleansing adventure, as I was too caught up in too much of what I perceived as urgencies. After all, I am now feeling way more at ease leaving some needs for action unattended, while working on something of bigger meaning, as for example this book. While this development provides the long-desired peace of mind, it comes with the positive side effect of achieving more, since we create impact not by getting many small things done but instead by accomplishing the few big ones that matter.

While my circumstances in Ibiza and Koh Tao had some important aspects in common, each of these lifestyles came with its own specific challenges, each of which provided its own particular food for thought. The previously discussed commonality of letting go of perceived responsibilities appears similarly important as having a television neither in Ibiza nor in Koh Tao. It was particularly the latter that triggered many of the positive developments discussed in this book, also the shift from doing to being. Even though I spent a certain portion of my old life unproductively, I still spent it doing, as I used television to keep my mind busy. Consequently, it was the absence of this distractor that helped me to move some of my focus inwards, spend my time more mindfully and, therefore, use it more meaningfully, even though it strongly felt as if I was making no use of my time. It is, however, this shift from doing to being which plays and important role in living a happy and fulfilled life. Whereas doing nothing felt boring and even got me restless at first, it provided exactly what was needed to let my thoughts flow and generate ideas and a vision for my future, once I had started to rest more in myself and be comfortable with going for an extended walk and not checking my phone once during the entire time.

Whereas these are the significant commonalities in each of the two major legs of my journey, they both had their own specific characteristics, each of which triggered specific developments with regards to "Spend Your Life Being Instead of Doing". We shall now look at each of them in some more detail.

When I am now looking back, my life in Ibiza and Koh Tao were significantly different, especially in one regard. My days and weeks in Ibiza were highly organized, as I was externally driven by the meticulous daily schedules by our management. These daily schedules did never contain any slack, which made the Sundays the first moment to calm down after a six-day work week. Every day was a struggle to not fall behind schedule and I did in no way live the laid-back lifestyle that I had envisioned when I dreamt of becoming a scuba diving instructor. It was my time in Koh Tao, which provided the lifestyle that I had dreamt of for so long, but it now appears to me as if the stressful time in Ibiza was exactly what I needed to get ready for the second leg of my journey. As will become obvious further down this book, my reflections and insights became much deeper and future-oriented in Koh Tao, which appears to be the result of a bigger distance to my old life as well as significantly more slack time. I have now come to understand that the stressful time in Ibiza was needed before going to Koh Tao, as I could break with some old habits and free my mind for deeper thinking.

First and foremost, it came as a great relief that my job implied spending my entire day outside, while working in or near the water made it impractical, if not impossible, to check my smartphone during the day. In my office job I was used to having it next to me all day and caught myself checking emails and social media every few minutes. In Ibiza, however, I checked my phone during breakfast but was hardly ever able to do so between 9 am and 5 pm. What stressed me at first, soon started to turn out as a great experience. It comes with no surprise that there have rarely been any interesting news after a few minutes, whereas in Ibiza I learnt to acknowledge that even after eight hours I had never missed anything, which was too late to deal with after the end of my workday. I never faced any negative impact of ignoring my phone for eight hours. In fact, the result was quite the opposite. Once you acknowledge the negligible amount of information gained from checking your phone every few minutes, it does not require a significant cognitive step to understand that all you do is in fact procrastinating what you should instead spend your time and focus on, even if this means simply living our life or allowing us the time to reflect and digest our experiences. As I was becoming more comfortable to check my phone less, I started to appreciate one more positive side effect of it. Whenever I check my phone without finding any interesting news, it triggers a small sense of dissatisfaction, even though it might remain unconscious and not reach my awareness. Checking my phone only after eight hours, on the other hand, comes with an increased likelihood of having received new messages and interesting inputs. It is, therefore, not difficult to understand how checking my phone less increased my overall satisfaction and contributed to living more mindfully in the moment.

It comes with relief but also some degree of regret that I did already know these things about the use of smartphones before I went to Ibiza. It is relieving to realize that I did not spend my last years entirely ignoring the obvious, but at the same time it fills me with some regret that I did not change my habits earlier. As it is possible but challenging to change our deeply embedded habits, it required externally imposed restrictions to come to a healthier use of my emails and social media accounts. It is, interestingly, another insight that proves the importance of leaving our comfort zone to grow as a person. While it is already difficult to break with a habit, it is even more difficult to embed the new way of doing things as a habit. Whereas I had broken the addictive and unhealthy relation with my smartphone in Ibiza, I started moving into the wrong direction again in Koh Tao. It turned out that one of the characteristics of my life in Koh Tao was counterproductive against my newly acquired habit, a challenge that I will reflect on in more detail a bit later. It will now be my challenge to not fall back into old habits and routines but to make sure to keep these insights and new practices for my future life. Therefore, it feels good and promising to maintain my focus on these pages in front of me, while my phone keeps vibrating a meter away. I, however, decided to ignore it for a while.

If we want to spend our life being who we are instead of doing what we believe we are supposed to do, it appears as a relevant question whether goals for our future are healthy or if we should rather sacrifice them for living in the moment. This is indeed a tricky question, as there is only a thin line between having goals to give us a purpose on one hand and allowing them to take control over our thinking and being on the other. As I have already indicated before, I have always been convinced and still am that having meaningful goals is important to give us a purpose and makes the difference between a mediocre and a fulfilled life. It is important, however, to not get so deeply caught up in working towards our goals that we forget living our life, which is essentially one of the most important meanings of our being. As we constantly balance and shift priorities between our various goals and dreams, we must not forget to recognize life itself as one of them.

Before I went to Ibiza, I saw everything that I did as something that had to be finished. Even if I spent my time on something which I was highly passionate about, such as scuba diving or teaching diving courses, parts of my attention were already with the next things I would have to do afterwards. I always felt in a hurry and hardly ever managed to just be, as I was constantly busy doing. A clear daily structure and a simple life in Ibiza started my progression towards enjoying life as the goal itself and not seeing it solely as the way to achieve something else. I started to indulge in the moment and allow things to take as long as they deserve.

When I am now comparing my thoughts and feelings in Ibiza with those in Koh Tao, it puzzles me to realize that one aspect, which I consider one of the major flaws of my time in Ibiza, now appears to be a significant contributor to my transition from doing to being. I have spent most of my diving career with SSI, but nevertheless chose another training agency's dive centre for my time in Ibiza. While I was aware of my preference for a SSI dive centre, when I took the decision by the end of 2018, it was the sum of all aspects, such as free movement within the European Union and expected more diverse lifestyle in Ibiza, that made Ibiza appear the best option out of the choices I had. Working for a different training agency's dive centre and, consequently, not getting formal recognition for half a year of my experience appeared as a minor concern, since developing as a person was my major ambition for my sabbatical. It was the teaching of SSI courses with the associated progress as a diving instructor in Koh Tao, however, that made me perceive my time in Ibiza as a waste of time. While I still regret that I could by now be further in my professional diving development, it was giving up on this opportunity in Ibiza, which supported me in developing a healthier mindset with regards to how I should spend my time.

As in Ibiza my issued certifications did not count towards my next SSI career step, my mind could easily focus on the diving and teaching as a purpose itself. I indulged in my passion and spent my time being a scuba diving instructor as opposed to doing the necessary towards my next goal. Whereas it did sometimes feel as a waste of time to not get my certifications recognized,

I do realize now how great a relief it felt to do something for the pure sake of doing it instead of achieving something. It was my thoughts and feelings in Koh Tao that make me realize this now, since during the second half of my journey my focus started shifting. I was getting increasingly motivated again by finishing my courses and the progress towards my next goal that was coming along with it, while I should have enjoyed the diving and teaching itself. I was becoming less mindful.

Taking this experience into account, we must understand the importance of life goals but also the importance to enjoy the new status once we achieved them. If we only achieve one goal to rush into the next one, we forget to enjoy life and get instead again caught in spending our entire life doing the necessary. After all, doing less but doing it mindfully leads to a life better lived than doing more without being able to enjoy it. There is, in simple terms, no rush. The full meaning of these thoughts becomes clearer, when I look at my intention in writing this book. Of course, I have a goal in mind and hope to finish and publish it at some point. It is, however, equally the process of writing that motivates me. Mindfully typing these lines is also a way of appreciating and digesting my experience and it feels great, when I get into the flow and fully indulge in what I am doing. It feels great if doing something becomes equally or even more important than getting it done and puts the desired result into the background.

While my transition from doing to being already started in Ibiza, it caught more momentum and became much stronger during my time in Koh Tao or, to be more precise, once I had settled and knew how long I was going to stay. Once my mind acknowledged the needlessness to rush through my days, especially with regards to handing out CVs to dive centres and getting to know people, I became much more at ease with doing what feels right at any given moment as opposed to what I thought I had to do. I started to feel a lot more comfortable to not have my days controlled by my to-do lists but live in the moment instead. I stopped caring about ticking as many boxes on my list as possible but enjoyed doing the things that matter, take me forward and make a difference. By now I can say that I have not recognized any negative consequences from writing this book or meeting people, while leaving several seemingly urgent topics unattended. In fact, it was a worthwhile experience to see that very too often the seemingly urgent activities ask for attention, while it is the non-urgent ones that take us forward. It is their dilemma though that the meaningful ones are usually coming without any pressure. It is, therefore, our responsibility to create the urgency they need.

To put the previous lines into an appropriate context, I need to clarify that I am far from populating the idea of being lazy or wasting our time. While many of us are so caught up in their daily hectic life that sitting down for reflections appears as laziness or a waste of time, it is the intentions and mindfulness that make it valuable and worthwhile. When we learn to acknowledge the importance and benefits of relaxing and reflecting, in other words being for a while instead of only doing, we will not only appreciate the positive impacts on our state of mind and health but will also see our effectiveness and productivity increase. It is usually in these calm and mindful moments that we start to see with more clarity and get a better sense of what our next priorities should be. Being able to let go is, therefore, not only important for avoiding psychological stress but also necessary for making effective use of our time. It should be obvious that instead of running in circles mindlessly it is way more successful to stop for a moment to reflect on where we are in relation to where we want to be and then continue mindfully into the right direction with a sharpened mind.

As I mentioned in the beginning of this chapter, I left Germany with the habit to reflect in the evenings on how productively I had spent my day. However, I hardly ever reflected on how mindfully I had lived that day or if I had appreciated the beautiful aspects of my life enough. It needed two triggers during my time in Ibiza to shift the focus of my reflections from how I have done to how I have been. Initially, I needed time to get used to the meticulous plans, by which our management determined what our days looked like. Until May 2019 I had always enjoyed being the one who defined how I spent the days in my professional as well as my private life. I still appreciate the freedom to spend my days as I want and enjoy it even more now that I have experienced the opposite. It was, however, this needlessness to reflect upon my priorities of the past day which helped me to spend more time thinking about my state of mind during the previous hours. Furthermore, it was to work as a scuba diving instructor, something I like and am passionate about, that made me reflect more upon if I was enjoying my work and life enough. As I had come to strongly dislike my 9-to-5 job by the beginning of 2019, it seemed mentally acceptable to focus on the negative aspects of my work and keep my spirit alive by the outlook that I would break free. Now that my dream had finally become true, however, I had to accept the question if I was enjoying it as I should. The insight came, unfortunately, very humbling and eye-opening, as I will reflect upon in the next chapter.

In a certain way it was another valuable challenge for me to leave the German structured and organized mindset behind and exchange it for the more laid-back approach in Spain and, even stronger, in Thailand. It may be a stereotype to some extent, but after working in project management for several years I felt most comfortable if everything was well structured and organized, with no room for flexibility and spontaneity. From my professional life I was used to having closure dates for every open topic including contingency plans for the case that something goes wrong. It is, however, the unexpected developments and happenings which provide us moments full of life, but we need to allow them to happen. Accordingly, this is an example of a work habit, which should not be allowed a big influence on our private life but that had taken over my private life way too much.

Since in my old life I was way too often not ready to let these unexpected moments happen, it turned out as a challenging but long needed lesson that I had to learn to let go of control, especially when I moved to Thailand. As I was moving to a country outside the European Union, I suddenly faced many new challenges and uncertainties and had many things to take care of, in a country where things work very differently than in Germany. At the same time, it was not long ago that I had returned home from Ibiza. I was, consequently, still waiting for documents and evidence of my employment in Spain, some of which I needed to provide to the German administration for them to take certain decisions. As these decisions were to have an influence on the further development of my financial situation, I was obviously very keen to close these topics soon and was getting the more nervous the longer it took. As it was, however, only a bureaucratic formality and it was clear what the outcome of these decisions would be, it was a relief to realize that it made no difference if the decisions were taken now or later. Since my financial buffer was big enough, the result would be the same in the long term. I was again not stressed for an actual reason but only by that part of my mindset, which dislikes open ends and enjoys getting things done. While the last year has certainly taught me in a powerful way the importance of letting go of control, I must nevertheless realize how big a room for improvement I still have in this regard. I am still impressed how easy-going and laid-back some of the people in Thailand, western people living there alike, are and they do in no way get along worse than any of the people living their stressful life in Europe.

Unfortunately, when I am now looking at one of my newly acquired habits during my time in Ibiza, it causes me some regret to realize a setback into an old habit during my time in Koh Tao. As I have discussed before, it came with great relief to ignore my phone for most of the day during the summer of 2019. Once I started to work freelance, however, it was one characteristic of this kind of working that made me check social media way too often again, every few minutes to be specific. As I learnt during my first weeks in Koh Tao, needs for freelancers were usually posted through job boards on social media and dive centres asked for my availability by text messages. They hardly ever called. It became apparent that they tended to approach several freelancers at the same time and, unless those who I had managed to build a strong connection with, it was the first one replying who would get the job. Obviously, it did not take long until I found myself constantly checking my phone again, as I was afraid of missing job opportunities. I had fallen back into one of the unhealthy habits which prevent the mind from living in the moment and enjoying the beauty of life. As I continued living my freelance life, however, I began to understand that my obsession with the job boards on social media was unnecessary for most of the day. I started to realize that most of the requests for freelance instructors appeared in the evenings, as I now understood when students signed up after the courses of the full-time instructors had reached their maximum number of participants. Consequently, I might have missed some job opportunities if not checking my phone regularly but taking into account the low number of requests before five o'clock the decrease of life quality and mindfulness outweighed the increased number of taught courses gained from constantly checking my phone.

While this insight contributed to my peace of mind to some almost negligible extent, it was towards the end of my time in Thailand that my mind started to relax and I could let go of my phone in order to indulge in what I was doing. Once I acknowledged that my return to Germany, as I assumed at that point, was approaching, I started to care less about financial sustainability and, accordingly, became more at ease with focusing for instance on reading a book on the beach whilst ignoring potentially missed opportunities to teach another course. During the last days before my flight to Europe

I developed a routine for the days when I was not teaching any courses, which I appreciated as healthy for my productivity as well as my mindfulness. After working on this book in different cafés for some time in the morning, I chose one of the island's many beautiful beaches to explicitly do nothing except for resting, thinking and reading a book for about two hours, before finding another café to work on one more thing in the evening. This daily structure turned out to provide two interesting and to some degree challenging experiences, which I hope to nourish from in the future.

Firstly, as it relates to the previous discussion, I forced myself to ignore my phone entirely while I was on the beach. Whereas it was challenging as the temptation to look at it grew stronger, it turned out as a powerful relief for my mind to feel the decreasing temptation as my brain started to let go and it came as an intriguing, nevertheless not surprising, insight that after two hours I had never missed anything of importance. Secondly, as it relates to spending our time on what matters, it turned out as highly productive and helped to achieve mindfulness to work on two meaningful tasks per day as opposed to rushing from one small task into the next. Resting on the beach in between to sharpen my mind certainly helped to be mindful during the second work slot of the day, as it focused my mind on the selected task and put anything else aside.

While I admit that it is easy to follow such a structure when living on a tropical island and not having much to take care of, I still consider these few days a healing experience which reminded me of some important principles that can make our daily professional and private life more productive and less stressful in the typical western 9-to-5 life as well. In some way, these days prepared me for my transition back to Europe. As the transition continues now that I have left the laid-back lifestyle of Thailand behind, but can still enjoy a few weeks off before starting my new job, I realize that I continue to follow these two habits, even though I am still adjusting them to my new environment and circumstances. I am, therefore, optimistic that I will be able to nourish from them for a long time, once I will start my new job.

It is intriguing to realize how it most often requires extraordinary periods in our life or extreme situations to bring these insights, which many of us already have deeply hidden in their unconscious mind, to the surface. As I am writing these lines at the time when the COVID-19 pandemic is spreading at maximum speed in most countries around the world, it comes with no surprise that some of my reflections create a link between Ibiza and Thailand as one of the most enjoyable periods of my life on one hand and one of the world's so far greatest challenges of the 21st century on the other. As we are currently forced to experience in a powerful, painful and not yet controllable manner, we as humans are far from able to plan for everything and have contingencies in place for whatever happens. Less than four months ago nobody could have anticipated that by spring 2020 the life, as we know it, would have been turned upside down and some of the most basic social and economic fundamentals overthrown. As life has come to a stillstand in many countries, we are forced to adjust how we live our life, give up on many of our habits and postpone some of our biggest life goals for a not yet known period.

While it will certainly require a significant time to reverse the impacts of the current pandemic, some of which might not even be reversible at all, it is our responsibility to decide with which mindset we approach this situation. This time teaches us in a powerful way that we need to learn to let go and let things happen, since we are far from able to control everything. While accepting what we cannot influence is an important prerequisite for mental health, I am nevertheless not populating that we should all re-sign from our ambitions. It does, however, serve us and others best if we make our contributions in a smart and reasonable manner and think about how to make best use of this time. Whereas it appears easy to surrender in grievance about the current restrictions and use them as excuse for mediocracy, we can as well use the new gained time for the things we used to neglect in our normal busy life. Personally, I could not imagine a worse timing for a transition into a new job. Although I am now happier than ever that in early 2020 I accepted my new job from 1st May, it is hard to predict what will happen in the next weeks. On the positive side, however, I would not have as much time to work on this book now, if my life would have developed as planned. I am certainly far from considering what is happening positive and would have wished for a different end to my time in Thailand, but I at least try to approach it with the most constructive mindset, if that is the best I can do.

When I now compare myself in April 2019 against the version of me by the end of March 2020, it makes me happy to realize that I have made a significant transition from doing to being. I feel more at ease to let things go, have my life less controlled by my to-do lists, do currently feel more comfortable to ignore emails and social media for a while and am more able to live in the moment and focus on what matters. Considering what these last eleven months triggered in me, I am convinced that this state of mind is a result of breaking loose from my regular life for a while. Looking at myself in April 2019 confirms how important and direly needed this side-track from the 9-to-5 rat race was for me. However, I also realize that by no means I can take these achievements for granted and how much room for improvement still exists. When I transferred from Ibiza to Koh Tao, I had to learn how easily we fall back into our old habits, if we do not stay alert and constantly challenge ourselves. Despite having learnt to entirely ignore my smartphone in Ibiza, I got highly dependent on it again and had to regain control in Koh Tao. It was an inspiration and taught me how much I can still improve, when I saw how easy-going and laid-back many of the people in Koh Tao are and, nevertheless, get along very well. Especially in these days of COVID-19 islands like Koh Tao and their inhabitants are much harder hit by lockdowns, as their entire existence is centred around scuba diving and tourism. It is, therefore, inspiring to follow how creative some of them are to move forward in this what might appear to be a desperate situation.

As it was to a big degree the laid-back atmosphere on a small tropical island like Koh Tao which triggered my transition from doing to being, it comes with no surprise that this long-needed relaxation of my mind manifested itself during my travel back to Europe. Since I wanted to eliminate the risk of something going wrong as much as possible, it was on purpose that I booked my trip so that I had to wait eight hours at Koh Samui airport for my flight to Bangkok, where I would have to wait another three hours until my connecting flight to Stockholm. I did it notwithstanding my awareness how much these waiting times would have stressed me in the past, even more as they meant waiting for another eleven hours of sitting on a plane. It was, therefore, a surprise and relief to realize that I did not mind these eight hours at Koh Samui airport at all. While it was partially due to having a purpose in writing this book and realizing that I could spend my time at Koh Samui airport similar to how I would have spent it at Koh Tao, it also helped that I had learnt to be comfortable with doing nothing for a while. Eleven months had changed me for the better.

Some might now consider me in a lucky position that I was able to go on this trip. As I, however, do by far not come from any rich or elite background, I am convinced that except for maybe very few real obstacles most people could do the same if they really want it and set their mindset right. Nevertheless, even those who might not be able to break loose can act to enrich their mindset and life. Among other ones I am taking two important experiences from my eleven months in Ibiza and Thailand. This time essentially provided me, on one hand, a trigger to challenge my status quo and, on the other hand, an incentive to surround myself with the right people to get the inspirations I desired. While breaking loose and living abroad certainly served as a catalyst for something I already knew but never really managed to make a habit, everyone can and should create the right circumstances and environment to find these two favourable factors. After all, it is not necessary to break loose entirely to go out and meet different people, change habits and try out new things and, maybe most importantly, make reflection and mindfulness a regular and consistent part of our life. Making these changes tends to be challenging at first. Surrounding myself by people way more extrovert and living an entirely different lifestyle than me was by far not always easy, but I realized that it is possible to become comfortable again and ultimately gained a lot from this experience.

Having gained so much from the last eleven months, it will now be my challenge to maintain this mindfulness and focus on being instead of doing, when I am starting a new life outside professional scuba diving. It is on purpose that I am not talking about returning into my old life, as I would then not have used the last year as I could. Making those new learnings a habit will certainly be challenging, when I start my new job, but it is with the same certainty that it is possible to live mindfully even in hectic and turbulent times somewhere else than on a small tropical island. I am, therefore, optimistic that my year as a scuba diving instructor has changed me for the better and has made me a more mindful person in the long-term.

4.3 Happiness Will Not Find You

A common discussion these days concerns the question what happiness means and how to achieve it. After all, our aim to be happy is one of the most important underlying motivators for almost all the things we do in our life. Even some of those daily routines, which we perceive as a burden rather than joy, are indirectly driven by our desire to be happy. Although many people do not like their jobs, most of them work more than they like to earn the money which is needed for a happy and fulfilled life. Some of our daily healthy habits are not driven by the joy they provide, but by our knowledge that they contribute to our health, which in return we need to live a happy life. As happiness is such an important quest for us as humans, it is worth having a look how it developed for me, when I left my 9-to-5 job behind and exchanged it for living my long-held dream of working as a scuba diving instructor for a while.

When I am now looking back to how it all began, I struggle to remember how exactly the idea of becoming a scuba diving instructor crossed my mind. I still remember when it appeared quite well though. It was during an inspiring vacation at the end of 2014 and beginning of 2015 when a friend of mine and I talked about our plans and resolutions for the upcoming year. By that time, I was a PADI Open Water Diver with very few dives under my belt and had not been diving for several years. My main goal was to go diving again, which meant that I repeated what I had been having as a goal for a long time but never managed to achieve, no matter how easy it would have been to find a dive buddy and get into the water again. As inconceivable as it appeared at that time, it did not take long until the idea to continue to instructor manifested in my mind. As much as I struggle to remember how exactly this idea crossed my mind, as clear it seems to me what the two main underlying motivations were. On one hand, as it relates to the previous chapter, I have always been and to some extent still am more motivated by doing something to achieve a goal rather than doing something for the pure joy of it. As such it felt great to have a goal, which I could achieve if I continued diving. On the other hand, I had a vision in my mind of me living a laid-back life in a beautiful sunny location, combining travelling, diving and teaching as three of my greatest passions. Consequently, my quest for happiness was the second big motivator to embark on this several years long project. It is not hard to imagine how much more appealing it is to work with happy people while wearing flip-flops and swim shorts than staring at my computer in a neon-lit office for 40 hours a week.

Soon after I started my six-months job in Ibiza I had to realize, however, that working as a scuba diving instructor does not automatically and necessarily make me a happier person. Without any doubt it offered me a huge potential to be happy, but I had to acknowledge that it remains my responsibility to think positive and appreciate the beautiful aspects of my life. After all, happiness is an internal mindset and choice much more than it is externally dependent on specific prerequisites. While life and work as a scuba diving instructor certainly is a great benefit which can contribute to living a happy and fulfilled life, I still had to choose to appreciate and adore it as much as it deserved. Whereas some people are happy despite the little things they possess and the simple life they live, others are highly unhappy notwithstanding the great life they are having. The favourable life does not automatically make us happy, if we have the wrong mindset and do not decide to allow it to do so.

I remember as if it was yesterday what I thought and how I felt when we were heading out for our first dive in Ibiza. I was overwhelmed by a flush of happiness and purely amazed by the realization that what felt like holidays would now be my daily life. I was sincerely happy and satisfied that I had achieved what I had been dreaming of for several years. It felt as if life could not be any better now that I had left my disliked job behind and would not have to sit in an office for at least six months. It is sad, however, that soon I started to take the beautiful aspects of my new life for granted and, accordingly, the overwhelming sense of satisfaction and happiness started to fade away. My focus started shifting from appreciation of the beautiful aspects of my life towards an unhealthy grievance about the flaws which unavoidably come with every life setup. In life there are hardly ever any gains without any associated costs.

Unsurprisingly, living a simple life on the beach earning my money as a scuba diving instructor comes with many beautiful aspects but requires certain sacrifices in terms of conveniences that I had gotten used to in my high-standard life in Germany. As soon as I started to take my new life for granted, I began to miss my sofa, my car and my privacy, to mention only a few of the things I had gotten used to in my life before May 2019. Ironically, until April 2019 I had been taking these things for granted and, therefore, not been appreciating them as much as I was missing them now. In fact, I did never even think about them. Instead, I had always been feeling a strong longing for those things which I was now starting to take for granted in Ibiza – being out in the sun all day, diving daily and meeting many interesting people, again to mention only a few. It was then in August that another interesting effect related to mindfulness became visible. As soon as I had taken the decision to continue to Thailand from November and booked the necessary flights, it became even harder to appreciate my life in Ibiza, as my mind started to focus on looking forward to this next leg of my journey. Instead of pushing myself to focus on the positive aspects it had now become easy for me to accept the negative ones, as I could consistently tell myself that everything would be better in a few weeks anyways.

Therefore, it is no surprise that the same development of thoughts and emotions happened as soon as I arrived in Thailand, even though I am only realizing it now that I am looking back. As well as I do remember my emotions when we were heading out for our first dive in Ibiza, I will not forget my thoughts during the bus trip from Bangkok International Airport to my hotel for the first night and, even stronger, when I started teaching my first course on Koh Tao. I was equally overwhelmed and amazed as six months earlier, but now it was a strong feeling that I had finally arrived where I should have been half a year ago. I was genuinely happy and felt sincere appreciation for the things which I had been missing in Ibiza and which I looked forward to now. Teaching SSI courses and getting the recognition which is necessary for my career progress, my own apartment with its associated privacy and the freedom which comes with working freelance are only a few examples. Unfortunately, it did not take long until my mindset started to progress into the same direction, as discussed for Ibiza above. Whereas my life remained great and became even better as I was becoming more established and got to know more people, my appreciation started to fade away and my focus on the little flaws increased as I began to start taking the good life for granted. Ironically, I hardly ever adored the privacy which I had been looking forward to for long, as I did not possess the peace of mind to stay home, while life was buzzling outside. On the more extreme and sad side, my appreciation for the freedom that comes with working freelance turned into a grievance about the uncertainty which unavoidably comes along as well. As discussed before, we need to decide if we want to trade freedom for security or the opposite. It even got to the point, when it was going so well for me that I had to refuse a significant number of jobs, but instead of enjoying being busy I got annoyed by not being able to take these additional courses. My awareness was more on the opportunities which I missed than on the courses which I was teaching.

When I now reflect on these experiences, they teach me two important lessons, which have already influenced my thinking for the better and will hopefully continue doing so even stronger. As an unlimited responsibility for my own life and happiness remains with me, even if I work as a scuba diving instructor, I must on one hand remain proactive to spend my time meaningfully and, on the other hand, have the right mindset in order to adore all the beauties which the related lifestyle certainly provides. It is on us, however, to recognize and appreciate them.

With all the digital temptations these days, social media and smartphones to mention only a few, it has become way too easy to procrastinate and postpone by endlessly browsing the internet without finding anything of interest instead of living our life and searching for experiences that provide us meaning and excitement. Unfortunately, this had also contributed to my daily use of time a lot before I broke loose for one year. In fact, knowing that I would soon embark on one of my greatest adventures made it even easier to procrastinate, as it provided the possibility to convince myself that there was no need to change anything, since everything would soon be better anyways. I essentially spent my time waiting for that day in May 2019, when I would leave my mediocre life behind and exchange it for the supposedly exciting and glamorous life of a scuba diving instructor, as I had observed it on so many of my diving vacations before.

Once the first excitement about living in Ibiza had passed, however, I had to realize that even as a scuba diving instructor I must accept ownership of my life and need to be proactive and creative in designing my free time. While the days from Monday to Saturday were heavily predetermined, as we were busy working until five and socializing with guests thereafter, it was on the Sundays when the sudden moment of peace hit me and I had to decide how I spent my time. From a principal perspective I had three options how I could spend my days. Firstly, as we were living on a beautiful beach in a sunny country, it would have been easy to enjoy life on the beach and let the day pass by while doing nothing specific. As I had, however, not yet come far with the transition described in the previous chapter, I found myself left with the other two options. Secondly, it was obviously also an easy opportunity to be proactive and engage in an activity of some kind and, looking back in all honesty now, the best free days were those when I took a bus to Ibiza Town to take an exploratory walk around the city, rented a scooter to explore some of the further away parts of the island or signed up for a guided e-bike tour that took me along some of the most beautiful beaches within a few hours. While these experiences left me happy and satisfied in the evenings and provided me energy for the upcoming week, it was way too often that I lacked this proactivity and found myself not doing anything on a Sunday. It was not the pure fact of doing nothing which made these days a waste of time, however. It was the fact that it was not my conscious decision to do nothing but my inability to take a decision what to do instead. Consequently, I spent my days regretting that I was not doing anything, while I might as well have enjoyed this freedom.

Once we understand the underlying driving forces of an unhealthy habit or mindset, it becomes much easier to change it. Therefore, it is worth a few lines to discuss what often prevents us from making worthwhile use of our time and, thus, being happy. I can by now easily identify the two paradigms which let me spend many of my days in grievance that I was not going out to explore Ibiza further. On one hand, even though I was not conscious about it at that time, I was unconsciously afraid of missing interesting moments within my peer group at the dive centre while being away and taking the risk that my day may not be as exciting as I had envisioned it. It is, however, an easy conclusion that waiting for things to happen leads to significantly more missed opportunities than taking the initiative and proactively seeking experiences. It is the fear of missing something greater, which way too often leads to indecisiveness, while the worst decision we can take is to not decide and commit at all. A certain risk affinity is necessary if we want to be happy, which I will discuss separately in a bigger context later in this book. On the other hand, as it relates to the previous chapter, it was that doing-centred part of me with its self-imposed need to always do something productive which held me back from living a being-centred life and doing something for the pure joy of it. Fortunately, I have by now managed to let go of this self-defeating mindset to a significant extend. After all, not doing much on a Sunday was not the problem itself. The lack of appreciation for it was what causes me regret, as it could have been highly enjoyable with the right mindset… and maybe a good book!

Whereas I had, as discussed before, developed a healthy connection with my smartphone during my time in Ibiza, I could very well observe again in Koh Tao how emails and social media contribute to procrastination and, consequently, making less meaningful use of my time. While it got me a little nervous but felt great after a while to entirely ignore my phone while I was working, it was in the quiet moments that I found myself endlessly and purposelessly scrolling through my phone, always in the search for that one exciting thing which would make my day. Obviously, it was hardly ever that I found it, so that by now I must acknowledge that all I did was procrastination. Even if it were not procrastination in its sense of avoiding an important but difficult task, I was at least distracting myself from answering the question how I could make meaningful use of my time. As everyone observes in their life every now and then, our desire to go out and have fun typically diminishes when being tired or in a depressed mood. Therefore, it is no surprise that the temptation to use social media as a distracter grew even stronger in these moments. Unfortunately, an associated increase of its negative effects came along accordingly and took me into a down loop, which it took a while to break out off. It is especially in these moments that doing nothing to relax respectively going out in order to create positive emotions is more important than ever. Constantly checking ones' smartphone, however, triggers exactly the opposite, when it comes with the small disappointments about not finding anything exciting. Consequently, it is even more important to resist the digital temptations when they are the strongest.

These insights are not entirely new, and I have been realizing these things long before my time in Ibiza and Koh Tao already. Being stressed in the typical western 9-to-5 lifestyle and potentially frustrated about it does, however, make it even more difficult to change unhealthy habits for the better. Therefore, my time outside the rat race provided me on one hand a different perspective on my life, which was a powerful aid to challenge my mindsets and habits, and on the other hand the spirit and free time to act on them. It was one specific experience which challenged my habits even more drastically than my sabbatical anyways did. It has become standard in the European Union nowadays and applies also when buying a local SIM card in Thailand, that free mobile internet data can be used anywhere. Therefore, it was a healing exercise to depend on Wi-Fi hotspots when travelling to other countries in Southeast Asia. Not being able to use the internet for most of the day forced me to make conscious use of it when connected and made me realize how I way too often use it unconsciously. In the past I way too often opened the internet browser on my phone in a somehow automated manner without even being fully aware of it.

I am now more successfully than ever following a routine, which I have been trying to implement for a long time. It feels like a great relief to set predefined time slots, one or maximum two per day, for checking emails and to ignore social media entirely unless I am receiving a push-notification about something of interest, for instance a private message. I have, therefore, achieved what I consider a healthy use, but will need to keep putting effort into keeping this new habit alive, especially when my daily stress level will rise as I will be starting my new job. Having left Asia three weeks ago, it feels good that my behaviour is still in line with these insights, but my short trips to Malaysia, Singapore and Vietnam have taught me another lesson. Whenever I started to relax back in my hotels in these countries, the temptation to endlessly play with my phone grew as I got connected to the internet again. Identifying unhealthy habits and consciously changing them is an important first step but turning the new behaviour into an unconscious habit is equally important while much more difficult.

As I have now elaborated on the need to be proactive in its meaning of not waiting for things to happen but accepting the responsibility to make meaningful use of our time, it is now time to discuss our responsibility to decide to be happy in more detail. After all, once we manage to add interesting activities into our time or consciously decide and accept to not do anything except for just being ourselves, we have everything it takes to be happy, if only we manage to appreciate what we have as much as it deserves. Doing things that are supposed to make us happy is only one side of the coin, while the even more important requirements for happiness are our mindset, attitude and philosophy. Happiness, as elaborated at the beginning of this chapter, is much more dependent on our internal mindset and decisions than it is externally dependent on facts and circumstances. Ultimately, it is us who must decide to enjoy what we have and do instead of focusing on what we miss. Otherwise, our negative mindset will always persist in focusing on flaws and avoiding happiness no matter how supportive our circumstances and lifestyle are. In this sense, breaking loose and working as a scuba diving instructor provided exactly what I had been dreaming of for long. I was living in a sunny place, went diving almost daily and was surrounded by happy, easy-going and inspiring people. The circumstances were perfect, and I had everything it requires for sincere happiness and satisfaction except for the right mindset. As soon as I started to take the beauty of my life for granted, I began to live less consciously and mindfully, and my focus shifted from enjoying my dream life to seeing the flaws.

It now causes me some regret when I acknowledge how beautiful life was during the last year and how little I appreciated it along the way. It is one of the lessons, which this year has taught me, that our tendency to take things for granted is one of the most important obstacles in our quest for happiness. I can recognize this tendency of mine a long way further back than the beginning of 2019. After graduation from university my first job was in consulting. I soon decided to leave it for my strong desire to settle down. However, it did not take long after starting a new job and settling down, when my desire to be on the road and travelling a lot began to grow stronger. While this newly risen longing for adventure appears to have favoured my motivation and effort to become a scuba diving instructor, my deeply embedded habit to take things in life for granted started to manifest in two ways soon after starting my six months job on the beach of Ibiza.

While I have already elaborated how my overwhelming emotions started to fade away after my first few days in Ibiza and Koh Tao, I can now that I reflect on it recognize one more impact on my happiness caused by taking things for granted. Despite all the satisfaction, which came with living on the beach in a sunny country, diving daily and inspiring others to also enjoy this hobby, my appreciation for this adorable life started to decrease and my desire for other meaningful activities to increase as time passed by. Whereas I felt comfortable about not doing anything except for relaxing and reading on my first Sundays in Ibiza, I started to feel an increasing restlessness and desire to do something when I began to take the diving increasingly for granted. In fact, life remained great and became even better as the weather got better, the ocean warmer and the beach busier, but it was again only my mind which resisted to adore these beautiful aspects of my life and decided to avoid happiness for focusing on the minor flaws. The weeks were still the same as before, but I did not acknowledge the satisfaction enough anymore for it to last for the Sunday. After all, every decision to go into a certain direction requires certain sacrifices and, no matter how great life is, we will always be able to find negative aspects, if we only search for them hard enough. It is, therefore, our decision whether we appreciate and enjoy the positive aspects or live with grievance about the negative ones.

Leaving a partly toxic environment behind and surrounding myself with positive, proactive and inspiring people was one of the key underlying motivators for each leg of my journey. While already before Ibiza I had felt that I had too many negative people around me and was, accordingly, hoping that I could change this for the summer of 2019, it was still a big part of my reason to continue to Koh Tao, as I felt that I was not as surrounded by happy people living the life I admired as I could yet. Therefore, I felt that I would miss out on something if not giving Koh Tao a try for several months. After all, I had already been to Koh Tao before and remembered it as one of the greatest vacations of my life so far, a big part of the reason for it being the inspiring people I met. Since the people we surround us with play such an important role in how we live our life and which mindset we adopt, these decisions seemed logical in order to become a happier person.

When I now reflect on this specific motivation of mine to live in Thailand for a while, I can easily and with certainty conclude that this expectation of mine has been met. During these four months I have met some of the most proactive, easy-going and positive people I have ever met. Hardly ever have I heard anyone in Thailand complain about anything, but instead did I experience a strong habit of seeing positive things in everything. The strength of the positive mindset of these people impressed me the most, when I was bidding my companions of the last four months goodbye, as I was leaving the island in a hurry due to the escalating COVID-19 pandemic. While in all honesty some people were simply refusing to acknowledge reality and that the emerging crisis would sooner or later also hit Thailand, which in fact it did with a nationwide lockdown going into effect only a few days after I left, it was impressive and eye-opening to see how some of them realized what was happening but nevertheless decided to keep their spirits high. Whereas many of even the long-term residents took the same decision as I and returned to their home countries before it was too late, many others decided to stay even after the dive centres as main income source as well as the bars and restaurants as the main leisure activities were forced to close down. It is impressive to follow how some of them still decide to be happy and adore the beautiful aspects of living on a small tropical island no matter how easy it would be to resign in grievance about not being able to go diving, which for many was not only the main reason to come to Koh Tao but also the only financial basis.

Being surrounded by all these strongly positive and optimistic people, while I still found myself bothering about the honestly small flaws instead of adoring all the beautiful aspects of living life as a scuba diving instructor in Thailand, makes me realize with even more emphasis our own responsibility to decide to be happy and avoid using our environment as an excuse not to be. Having left Germany, where I had used the fact of some people being negative as an excuse to have that same mindset, I was now where I had been wanting to be for several years and was now living in exactly that future, which I had for several years used as an excuse for procrastinating a change of my mindset towards a healthier one. Consequently, my life in Thailand was full of potential for happiness, but I learnt how difficult it is to change long-held habits and deeply embedded paradigms. Even though I had exchanged my toxic environment for the highly positive one, which I had been dreaming of for a long time, happiness did not find me automatically, as mindfulness and a conscious effort remain necessary to be happy. It is no surprise, however, that I was not able to change my attitude and way of thinking from one day to the next.

Nevertheless, I can conclude with certainty that my six months in Ibiza and four months in Thailand have pushed me a big leap forward on my path towards a more mindful and happier life. As it applies to many of the challenges and journeys in our life, the first step is usually the hardest, and these ten months have been the eye-opener to trigger important insights, which were necessary as a first step. It would be naïve to believe that from there on everything else will be easy and it will certainly require persistence to not fall back into old habits at least and make further progress at best. However, once the first step has been done, the temptation to procrastinate decreases significantly, as at least for me it is much easier to keep a momentum alive than to get a momentum at first. Therefore, it fills me with optimism to realize first improvements of my mindset in the sense of an increased appreciation for the positive aspects of my life. It makes me optimistic to realize that I feel a significantly decreased sense of regret, when I am missing out on opportunities, which I sacrifice with my decision to do something else instead. Whenever I find myself tempted to fall back into this old thinking pattern of mine, I now take a step back and take a moment to reflect whether this seemingly missed opportunity is worth the regret. In most cases, however, it turns out that it is not and that my doubts are only triggered by that persisting part of my personality which is constantly afraid of missing things.

As extraordinary times are usually the mind-changing ones, it is no surprise that yet another example is triggered by the current lockdowns due to the prevailing corona-virus crisis, in which I can realize a manifestation of the insights elaborated above. As I am writing these lines from Sweden, where life continues comparably close to normal, I am facing the outlook that I will soon have to return to Germany, where the economic and social life have been forced into almost non-existence. Obviously, my first reaction was that I was not looking forward to going back to Germany at all, while a second thought changed my perspective. With my strong tendency towards the more introvert end of the range of possible personalities, social life has never been a prevailing part of my life anyways. My first reaction was, therefore, not justified but again only caused by that part of me which always focusses on what I am missing instead of what I am having. This insight from the second thought becomes even more healing and powerful, as it provides me the peace of mind to make use of my time in isolation. After all, this time offers us a never seen opportunity to work on some of our long-neglected goals and projects, as it for example gives me more space to work on this book than I ever had in my life. Whereas it was always easy to maintain focus on my work on this book in Thailand, especially when an increased peace of mind came along with the approaching end of my stay, it is now getting increasingly difficult in the presence of seemingly important matters to take care of. While I could have easily set aside the same amount of time, it is easy to imagine how much effort to maintain focus it would have required in Germany, where I would have been tempted to go into town instead. I am far from promoting that the current situation is positive, but getting through these challenging times certainly gets easier, if we try to see some of its potential instead of resigning into grievance about what we miss. The second thought has proved to be very useful, as it made me realize that despite the current restrictions my life would not look so much different after all. The increased peace of mind and focus due to the elimination of tempting alternatives, however, makes a significant difference, as it does not only increase productivity but also happiness when regret about my decisions fades away, as there are not many alternatives to staying at home and getting things done. These difficult times in 2020 signify stronger than ever the importance of making best use of our time, appreciating what we have and critically reflecting if regrets about missed opportunities are justified or only the impact of a destructive mindset. As easy as it now may be to use the circumstances as excuse, the decision to be happy remains our responsibility.

Looking back at a similar experience in 2008 assures me that these insights and increased positivity are immediate results of leaving my bubble and changing my environment for some time. In 2008 I lived as an exchange student in Australia for eight months, a country where the people possess an impressively easy-going mentality. Consequently, the attitude towards life in Australia and on Koh Tao turned out as highly comparable. As not only the mindset of the people around me but also my own personal challenges were similar during these two periods of my life, it is no surprise that also my thoughts and feelings upon my return to Europe were alike. It strikes me to see how each of these two times in my life turned out as a catalyst to cut my roots and spread my wings. Until the end of 2007 my life had been highly linear, straight-forward and well within the perceived expectations of parents and society, as I rushed from high school through mandatory community service into university, where my focus remained on achieving good grades. It was these eight months in Australia, which taught me the important lesson that life happens outside this fast-forward career path. Consequently, I came back as a changed person with a free mind, who at that point did not know yet how much I was going to live and experience in the years to come, as I had opened for opportunities outside the beaten track. I already felt a strong Australian influence on my mindset, however, as I worried less and lived with the belief that things will turn out good anyways.

Unfortunately, the inspirations from Australia lasted only a few years before I started missing what I did not have. Having done many extracurricular activities outside the beaten track and, consequently, created a huge amount of lasting memories for a few years I started developing a strong desire for settling down in order to create structure and routine in my life. Considering the key points of this chapter, however, it is no surprise that it did not take long after achieving routine that I began to feel a desire for the opposite and wanted to break loose in order to live off the beaten track again. As I had, unfortunately, lost my wings, gotten deeply rooted and stuck in my comfort zone and straight-forward career path again, it took me until 2019 to take the next long overdue step out of my comfort zone and into a life, which would create valuable lasting memories. As I am now writing these lines four weeks after my return from Thailand, it fills me with satisfaction to realize that Ibiza and Thailand have had the same effect on me as Australia 12 years ago. It makes me optimistic to feel the same positive mindset as well as an equally big inspiration and motivation to not fall back into a society-imposed mediocre life, as I managed to cut my roots and spread my wings again. Therefore, I can now conclude that these side-tracks in our life have an important healing impact and can, consequently, be particularly important to repeat in certain intervals. What I have planned as a once-in-a-lifetime adventure will now be repeated in some time. Even if it may not have an equally significant effect of breaking loose, it will certainly inspire me again in many ways and challenge my way of thinking into a more positive direction.

4.4 Take Full Ownership of Your Life

As already elaborated earlier in this book, it is our fear of failure which holds us back from many exciting opportunities and developments in our life. If we, however, always give in to this fear and never take the courage to step into the unknown, this fear will ultimately also hold us back from living our life at first. It is this deeply embedded desire for structure and risk avoidance together with another common paradigm that often leads to living a life in mediocracy and keep dreaming our dreams instead of living them. I have experienced it myself how much easier it is to blame our environment and circumstances than to accept an unlimited and full responsibility for how our life goes. As I had gotten used to living a highly structured and secure life for several years until May 2019, the decision to break loose, step into the unknown and start an entirely different lifestyle became one of the most scaring decisions of my life. It, however, also turned into one of the most powerful lessons of my life, as it taught me the true meaning of accepting an unlimited responsibility for our life and that, no matter how big a risk we decide to take, there is always a way back.

While I was only little nervous in spring 2019, when my departure to Ibiza was approaching, I hardly slept the nights before my flight to Kuala Lumpur for my onwards travel to Koh Tao. This may appear a little irrational when considering that I had been to Koh Tao before and, consequently, knew what to expect, whereas I had absolutely no idea what Ibiza would look and feel like. It may appear even more irrational when adding the fact that I was leaving my old life when going to Ibiza but had already broken loose in November 2019. It was another difference, however, which caused these different feelings. In Ibiza I had a job with a predefined start and end date, accommodation provided by the dive centre and the security that my dive centre's management would guide me through the necessary bureaucratic arrangements. In Koh Tao, on the other hand, I only had an apartment and a pile of CVs but had to set up a new life from scratch and find a job, when my knowledge about life on the island was limited to that of a tourist. In other words, I was on my own and fully responsible for starting a new life, while in Ibiza things would have worked out even if I had waited for things to happen. I was forced to be proactive, whereas before Ibiza despite my ambition to be proactive my inner peace resulted from the unconscious and not acknowledged anticipation that I would not fail either, even if I did not manage to make the step from reactivity to proactivity. It is now intriguing to realize that it was exactly this need for proactivity and designing a new life which made Koh Tao the rewarding experience and life-changer it was.

Besides my time in Ibiza and Thailand, I had several other periods of my life which required me to accept risk and an unlimited responsibility for how my life goes. My exchange semester in Australia as discussed in the previous section was certainly one of them, my year as a member of the international board of a pan-European student organization another. As different as they all were, they all had two major aspects in common. On one hand, they all scared me as they required me to step into the unknown and leave many of my established routines behind, but on the other hand provided me lasting memories from periods in which I lived my life to its fullest as well as some of the most powerful triggers for further developing my personality. As I am now reflecting those great times of my life, I can easily recognize a strong transformation of my mindset and personality towards the better, when I compare before and after each of these periods. Those times, when I was living the structured and society-expected life well within the beaten tracks, in contrast, have merely passed by neither creating lasting memories nor developing me towards a stronger and more confident person. It is in fact the opposite, as I can easily identify the majority of my unhealthy thought patterns and habits result from these periods within the beaten tracks. Therefore, it is an easy conclusion how accepting an unlimited responsibility for my life and a certain amount of risk has been and will always be an important factor in keeping my life attractive and my spirit alive.

"If your dreams don't scare you, you aren't dreaming big enough." It was this quote of Ellen Johnson Sirleaf, 24th president of Liberia and first elected black female president in Africa, by which a friend of mine inspired me before my journey to Ibiza. When I am now looking back over the last few years and compare my goals in January 2015 with where I am now, this quote has proven to be very true. These last few years have taught me a very powerful lesson that one should never be afraid of dreaming and aiming too high. They also emphasized impressively how the smallest steps can trigger great life-changing developments. As mentioned earlier in this book, one of my new years' resolutions for 2015 was to go diving again after I had not been diving for several years after my Open Water Diver course in 2008. When I am looking back in all honesty now, it was exactly my risk-aversion and my unconscious refusal to accept responsibility for my life which were holding me back from doing what I had been dreaming of for several years. It was my very own lack of proactivity which prevented me from one of the greatest and most exciting developments of my life, as great things hardly ever appear out of waiting for them to happen.

Consequently, things started going into the right direction, when I stopped using my environment and my lack of dive buddies as excuses and put myself into the driver's seat of my life instead.

In fact, it was one very small step which set the base for the impressive changes and developments of the years that followed. It took a significant amount of time for me to overcome my hesitation to sign up for my Advanced Open Water Diver course in 2015, as it required a commitment to something that lay outside my comfort zone. When I finally worked up the courage to do it, it was still far beyond any possible imagination that this would only be the beginning of a journey which would lead me to working as a scuba diving instructor in Ibiza and Thailand for almost one year less than five years later. While my dream to go diving was ambitious enough to scare me back in 2015, I have now experienced and learnt that I could and should have dreamt much bigger and higher, as the scariest dreams are the ones most worth to be pursued. Since it does obviously not get me nervous anymore to go for a dive and even taking on responsibility for the safety of people who have never been underwater is becoming normal, these last few years are also an impressive manifestation of how comfort zones grow if you challenge their boundaries and get comfortable to take steps outside them. If we, on the other hand, do not work up the courage to challenge ourselves, we will miss out on many of the most exciting developments of our life.

While the need for proactivity and the power of small steps should by now be obvious, another intriguing insight results from my progression between January 2015 and April 2020. Even when I had signed up for my Advanced Open Water Diver course and the first thoughts about becoming a Divemaster had emerged, I was still planning terribly slow in little steps. My goal was to complete two of my Advanced Open Water training dives in 2015 and complete the course the year after, in which I aimed for doing 25 dives to slowly build up the experience necessary to become a Divemaster. While this plan seemed to me extremely ambitious at that time, I suddenly found myself finishing my course within six weeks and doing 74 dives until the end of 2016, all of this without any conscious effort to push for acceleration or any sacrifices in other areas of my life. Therefore, this journey is not only a story of dreaming high and that everything is possible, but also an example and lesson of how much we can achieve in a short period of time, if we listen to our passion and let it drive us to give what it takes while not fearing to step out of our comfort zone. We should, consequently, never limit our dreams or underestimate our ability to achieve them quicker than might seem feasible at first.

Reflecting on my journey of the last five years reminds me of a saying which I learned from my manager in one of my previous office jobs. "How do you eat an elephant with chopsticks?" was his usual reply when we found ourselves facing a task which seemed too big to complete. As ridiculous as the answer to this metaphoric question might seem at first, it proves absolutely true in the context of this book... "Little by little". While its more practical interpretation as it refers to how you organize yourself given a huge task is more obvious, it further unveils its deeper and more philosophical meaning when I reflect on it in the light of my experience of the last five years. Even after deciding to continue all the way to scuba diving instructor this decision of mine still scared me a lot and I was in no way confident that I would make it. It was not even the idea itself but the number of steps to get there. Although I had broken it all down into individual steps and could clearly see the way to achieve my goal, I was scared by the thought of getting stuck at some point and not making it all the way for whatever reason. The fear of failing along the way and feeling like a loser against my own standards was trying to hold me back and force me into a mediocre life. It is exactly this paradigm which prevents many people from setting themselves ambitious goals. I have now made it my guiding principle to never let it stop me from aiming high, since not trying at all is the only decision which will for sure lead us to failure. Even if I had dropped out of my journey for whatever reason, I would have been in no way worse off than before. It would still have been worthwhile, as I would have met a lot of interesting people, had a lot of fun and become a better diver along the way. While I am promoting the idea that every small step matters, I am of course very happy that I made it all the way to where I am now. However, we must never allow our fear of failure to hold us back from our big dreams and ambitions.

Furthermore, not being able to anticipate all consequences of our decisions must never be our excuse for indecisiveness. Since there are so many interdependencies in life that we can never grasp all of them, we must accept to make decisions on limited information, let things happen and accept unanticipated consequences which we are unable to foresee. When I was approaching my Instructor Training Course in Thailand at the end of 2018, I had a decision to make between quitting my job before the course to stay in Thailand right away on one hand and returning home to look for a dive centre abroad afterwards on the other. As risk averse as I was, it is no surprise that I decided for the latter, but I do now believe that it would have enhanced my experience if I had gone all-in. However, I was too afraid of something going wrong during the course so that I would find myself with neither a job nor a diving career. Thinking about this decision in honesty now, however, the risk of screwing my life was extremely low, as I had a financial buffer big enough to cover the time it would take to get back into the corporate world. I would, therefore, now do it different with the experience I have gained by now.

Nevertheless, while on one hand my decision was detrimental in the sense that it prevented me from staying on Koh Tao right away and made me miss some of the experience, on the other hand it prevented me from a less favourable path as already elaborated in chapter 2. After all, the timing of my Instructor Training Course together with my risk-aversion and the notice period to quit my previous job were the reasons why I did not sign the contract which I was offered by a major cruise ship operator. Without these constraints I would have gone for a step, which as I know now would not have been in my favour for the reasons which I have discussed earlier. Looking at these favourable and adverse impacts, this decision of mine in 2018 turned out as a very powerful experience of all the interdependencies of every decision we take and that we can never fully anticipate what any possible alternative is good for or bad. I am, therefore, happy that I took my decision as I did, since not taking a decision at all would have been much worse.

While I now consider myself a little wiser than one year ago and will certainly do some things a bit different when I embark on such a journey again, I am more than happy that I worked up the courage to break loose and live off the beaten tracks for one year. I had to overcome some doubts, but I am glad I listened to my own desire and took charge of the course of my life instead of giving in to social expectations. In fact, when I broke loose at the age of 34 after being part of the corporate world for seven years, I experienced an entirely different set of reactions compared to when I took the decision to go to Australia for my exchange semester. I was also confronted with envy and scepticism in 2007, but my decision was easy to justify, since it was somehow essential for students to study abroad for some time to enhance their resumes. When I informed the people around me about my decision to go to Ibiza, however, many of them comprehended this step much less. Although not explicitly expressed, it was obvious that some of them considered me unresponsible, as according to their mindset people of my age are supposed to be established in their work and remain so until they retire. It was the reaction by a companion of mine that so clearly and strongly emphasized our different world views. His question whether I planned to ever work again in my life was such a strong disregard of the fact that I was going to Spain for a full-time job with 48 hours a week. My idea of life did just not fit into the common belief that we are supposed to follow a predefined path from birth to retirement and every change is an indication of a lack of discipline.

As tempting as it became to refrain from my plan considering these reactions and doubts, as much happier I am now that I held on to my vision. It turned out that breaking loose from social expectations to live one's own life is not only one of the most difficult but also one of the most important and fulfilling mental progressions. Looking back at my own mental state at the beginning of 2019, I took one of the best decisions of my life and I was in dire need of such a journey to resharpen my spirit, as I was so strongly getting sucked into the very same mediocre and narrow view on life. I have now experienced again how going a little extravagant every now and then contributes a lot to enriching one's view on the world and life itself. All those periods of my life in which I felt alive, learnt to rest in myself, developed a vision for my future and consequently grew as a person have one thing among others in common. They all made the people around me consider me a maniac to some extent, but also made them feel a lot of envy. As I will now reflect how much I have benefitted from having to start from scratch in Ibiza and Thailand, it will become obvious how important it is to follow our own idea of how we want to live instead of blaming our environment for what is going wrong in our life.

Once we are established in our work, life and relationships, it becomes very easy to get stuck in a mediocre life, as the pain and need to create something are fading away. As soon as we have everything which it takes for a decent life, we become way too much at ease with spending our evenings watching television instead of following the proactive path of going out and discovering what life has to offer. While it may appear as the recipe for an easy life and not putting any of our achievements at risk, this reactive lifestyle is also the shortcut to looking back in regret when we are older, feeling sorry for all the great opportunities we missed in our life. I like to compare it with the workout regime, which we follow to stay fit and healthy. We might well satisfy our conscience and maintain a sufficient level of fitness if we give in to our lazy mindset and follow the same routine over and over. Running the same five kilometers track in 30 minutes every second day will certainly provide its contribution to the prevention of gaining weight and will with the same certainty make that part of our personality happy which adores comfort and routine. However, after doing this for a while, this workout will maintain our status quo but not take us any further. To trigger continuous physical growth, we must create new pain by changing our workout regime and adding activities, which our body is not used to. While in workout the pain is physical in the sense of sore muscles, it has a more metaphorical meaning, when we talk about our personal growth and progression in the wider context of life. Nevertheless, the underlying principle is the same. Therefore, I am happy that I created such metaphorical pain for me at the beginning of 2019, as it required me to take action and, consequently, grew me as a person.

Until April 2019 I lived a well-established life, which provided me a lot of stability, security and ability to plan. I had a highly paid and safe job, a decent apartment, a loan-free car and a social environment in which I felt comfortable, as I had been part of it for many years. In the discussed metaphor of the workout I had been running the same five kilometres for years and was, consequently, feeling comfortable and maintaining the status while, however, not making any significant progress. Even though the direly needed change and metaphorical pain was not my core motivation to go to Ibiza and Thailand, it now fills me with satisfaction that it turned out as one of the main outcomes. Therefore, it is great that my psychological need for goals, which can be partially counterproductive as discussed in section 4.2, made me go on this journey in the first place, as it triggered many valuable developments.

While in Ibiza it was highly tempting and easy to become reactive and let life flow considering the externally made arrangements as discussed before, in Thailand I had to start from scratch and the responsibility to create a lifestyle rested entirely with me. Whereas this responsibility made me highly nervous and anxious at first, it taught me a direly needed lesson in proactivity. For the first time in many years the common phrase "One day I will…" which had been an integral part of my previous life did not work anymore and I had to replace it with "I will… no matter what it takes", as I could not rely on the established routines of a mediocre life anymore. The same change in paradigms had already proved as an immensely powerful trim tab at the beginning of 2015, when I changed from "I would really like to go diving again" to

"This year I will go diving again". As it is, however, easy to revert into reactive behaviour during four years of living a well-established life, it turned out as a highly valuable experience to step off the beaten tracks, need to fix my life and build up something from scratch. As it is no coincidence that I started writing this book during my flight to Bangkok, another outcome of quitting my old life is worth to be mentioned. Most of my reflections and insights would not have unveiled their full impact if I had not gone on this adventure. In a well-established life it is way too easy to close one's eyes against the things which are going wrong. I could only get ready to confront the flaws of my life by removing the distractions which I used to hide them. Therefore, going to Thailand with close to nothing was one of the best decisions of my life, as it forced me to take an honest look at myself and my life and to take the necessary actions for improvements.

Every decision to go into a certain direction in life requires us to sacrifice alternatives. It should be obvious that I left many people and other parts of my life behind when I departed to Ibiza and Thailand and that it was certainly not easy. Unfortunately, it is the fear of losing some things, which causes indecisiveness for many people way too often. However, when we honestly look at it, there should not be anything wrong about giving up certain aspects of our life, if it is for the better. Even if things do not work out as planned, there is highly likely a way back if we have planned wisely and left some basic safety nets in place. One of the main things which I sacrificed, and which many people criticized me for jeopardizing, was the security of the life I had achieved. However, as by the beginning of 2019 I had built up a sufficient safety net in the form of financial savings, I was able to place a high value on personal freedom. Therefore, I did indeed sacrifice security to some extent, but I did so for the better. Whereas my thoughts and focus, consequently, shifted more towards worrying about my financial situation, the rational part of my brain knew that I would not be ruined even if things turned out entirely different than planned. I only had to remind myself of this fact every now and then.

Unfortunately, in life security and freedom are negatively correlated. The more security we want to achieve, the more freedom we need to be willing to sacrifice. The same holds true in the opposite direction. It is impressive how strongly I experienced this paradigm over the last twelve months. Before Ibiza my life contained a high degree of security but a comparably low level of freedom. I could rely on my monthly fixed salary, which was sufficient to pay the monthly rates for all kinds of insurances and pension funds. It was easy to foresee what was going to happen during the next months and to plan ahead. This security, however, came with the cost of having to spend Monday to Friday in the office and having to ask my employer for permission whenever I needed a day off.

While the tendency towards security still prevailed in Ibiza, I sacrificed it in Thailand for the sake of freedom. It felt great to do whatever and go wherever I wanted without having to ask anyone for permission to take a day off, but it of course required me to accept letting go of the security from a fixed monthly income. It was, however, this actual freedom which provided me also the mental freedom necessary to gain deeper insights and reflections about my life. While the ones in Ibiza were mainly practical and relatively superficial, the ones in Thailand went much deeper and provided me significant ideas and a vision for what I want to do with the rest of my life. I am, therefore, happy that I sacrificed my security for a while and exchanged it for the freedom which helped me to develop the vision that I was looking for. The last twelve months have taught me the important life lesson that we should never subordinate everything else to security, but that we should instead be proactive in taking calculated risks to live the life we desire. If we allow our need for security to be superior to everything else, we enter the shortcut to mediocracy and will most likely have to deal with regrets of some kind at some point.

Besides my financial safety net, it was another factor, which made it psychologically easier for me to break free from my structured life and go on this journey. Several years ago, I have written a personal mission statement for myself and I still keep it as an aid to guide me through the turbulent times of nowadays' life. The idea behind this very personal document is to clarify for myself my most important values and beliefs and remind me of them whenever I feel that I am getting disconnected and when I must take major life-changing decisions. Since it is supposed to contain my most fundamental values, it is not about my goals for the coming years, since they will hopefully be achieved and need to be redefined when their time has come. My mission statement does instead contain those of my beliefs, which I want to be eternal and guide me through life, independent of external factors and circumstances. It is the redline to keep life's inevitable turbulences as challenges but does not allow them to move me around like waves do with a tiny boat in the middle of the ocean. It, therefore, supports me in keeping control over my life and maintaining my proactivity instead of becoming externally driven and living a reactive life.

I have now understood that it was the perfect fit between my sabbatical and my mission statement, which allowed me to easily justify this adventure against my own personal standards. If it had been part of my values and goals to make an impressive corporate career, my year off would not have fit into my mindset and it is very likely that I would not have managed to convince myself to do it. However, since I do see work and my career as a means to enable a fulfilled life rather than the purpose of life itself, my time in Ibiza and Thailand connected well with my mission statement, as it served among others my ambitions to regularly step out of my comfort zone and progress in those of my hobbies which tab into my passion. It did, obviously, serve my ambition to advance as a scuba diving instructor very well. It is on purpose that throughout this entire book I am not calling this period of my life a side-track. It would have been a side-track or detour if it had been a break from achieving such goals like an impressive corporate career. However, this was not the case and it even did not only serve my scuba diving related goals, but also helped me to develop a vision for my future. It has, therefore, become part of my linear life path much more than a side-track, as it has prevented me from losing my vision and going off track as well as it has helped me to progress in my personality and life much more than it delayed anything. Keeping this in mind it became much easier for me to accept that this time used some of my savings, well knowing that it would not ruin my pension. After all, this adventure had been one of my financial goals, which I defined several years ago.

By now I have elaborated a lot on accepting ownership for our life and proactively adding meaningful and inspiring activities into our time. I faced another challenging question in this context soon after scuba diving as my main hobby so far had turned into my profession. During my first weeks in Ibiza it still felt as if I was getting paid for exercising my hobby, but despite still being fun it started to feel more and more like a profession, once the first excitement was gone. While scuba diving had been a significant part of how I spent my salary in Germany until April 2019, after a few weeks in Ibiza I felt an increasing desire to do something meaningful with my free time, even though it was usually only one day per week. Scuba diving as my main hobby so far had turned into my profession and so I was in need of finding something new for my free time. Therefore, it appears useful to discuss in some more detail my reflections and insights from this year in terms of how a big a variety of hobbies is useful. One might now argue that turning our hobby into our profession is a comparably extreme scenario and not relevant for many people. However, it becomes a relevant discussion for a wider group of the population, when we consider other developments which can trigger the need for a new hobby. Scuba diving is probably one of the best examples for an activity, which our health conditions can prevent us from doing from one day to the next and the first months in 2020 have shown how unexpectedly dive centres and dive sites can be locked down for several weeks due to a virus, which nobody could have foreseen some months ago.

There is a thin line between relying on a too small variety of hobbies on one hand and adding too much into our life on the other. As elaborated earlier in this book, one of the best experiences in Ibiza and Thailand was letting go of some of my commitments and, consequently, adding more free time and flexibility into my life. I have learnt that adding too many activities into our life is not a good idea, no matter how much fun they are. As soon as we sacrifice relaxing and digesting our experiences for the sake of experiencing more, all these supposedly exciting activities turn into meaningless entries in our busy schedules. Being under constant time pressure and struggling to get everything done, will sooner or later decrease the appreciation for our hobbies and the joy we will get from them. We will stop being and start doing instead. On the other hand, however, relying on one hobby only is likely to make us bored and, therefore, also lead to a decreased sense of appreciation. Hence, the question how many hobbies we need does not only become relevant, if we turn our hobby into our profession, are confronted with new health conditions or simply become older. Having diverse sources of inspiration also keeps us energized and our spirit alive under normal circumstances. Ironically, my increased amount of free time in Ibiza and Thailand triggered two thoughts, which may appear mutually exclusive at first. Whereas this reduction of perceived obligations was direly needed in a first step, it made me realize that I need to find more passions besides scuba diving in a second step. Sometimes we need to clean up our life to create space for something new. Therefore, it is not only a question of finding the right balance between too few and too many activities, but also a challenge of finding activities, which we are passionate about and which will, thus, keep us energized rather than just busy.

Whereas my struggles in Ibiza and Thailand mainly related to needing a change from scuba diving now and then, my reflections and insights about my need for more hobbies became much more powerful during the 18 days, which I spent home in November 2019. As I had highly overestimated the effort to prepare for Thailand and scuba diving respectively other activities with friends were difficult, because everyone else was working, I soon found myself bored and asking myself what I can do with my time. My thoughts even went to the extreme that I started wondering how to spend my time after retirement in more than 30 years if I am already getting bored after 18 days without a job now. These thoughts and questions were bothering me a lot at first. However, it turned into a healing experience that I was suddenly forced to deal with questions, which I had been denying with a charade of unfulfilling activities for several years. Sometimes it requires the removal of distractors to face the ugly truth. After all, these challenging and quiet weeks have triggered my creativity, so that I have now not only revived some of my ideas from years ago but also come up with new interests which I would not have thought about a year ago.

It fills me with happiness and motivation to realize that these months abroad have triggered new passions and hobbies in me, which I suspect to be a direct result of my transition from doing to being as described earlier in this book. It was this transformation from doing things due to feeling obliged to do so towards doing what feels right at any given moment, which acted as the catalyser for new passions to grow. During the last few years I could already observe an interest of mine for photographing extraordinary sceneries, even though it was apparently only a side effect of my passion for scuba diving much more than a passion itself. Whenever I went diving at spectacular spots, I usually had my action camera with me, always on the lookout for extraordinary sceneries, which only scuba divers can find. The attentive and mindful reader might already have gotten stuck with the word "action camera" as an indication that I have so far not been a very sophisticated photographer. Instead of considering myself an underwater photographer so far, I have rather been a random diver with a camera. In fact, it took some very pragmatic thoughts to move the photographing itself into the spotlight. Looking for some extra cash flow for times of not getting much freelance work in Thailand I started getting more and more into stock photography. While I am not naïve enough to assume that it will provide the passive income for my financial independence, it has at least raised my awareness for the joy of searching for the perfect picture. Whereas my photography during the last few years has been almost entirely limited to underwater, my interest has now extended to looking out for special moments and sceneries on land as well. Therefore, it is no surprise that I now find myself with good photography equipment on my shopping list and an eagerness to develop from random snapshots to a conscious hobby and increasing my stock photography portfolio. Fortunately, it goes hand in hand with scuba diving and travelling as two of my other passions and may even create some extra cash if I put some effort into taking great pictures and marketing them well.

However, my newly discovered interest for photography is not the only result of my reflections and insights from this special period of my life so far. Several years ago, before I revived scuba diving as a hobby, I was considering several options how to spend my time and money of the years to come. Obtaining a private pilot licence for small motorized airplanes was one of them, because I have always been passionate about aviation for as long as I can remember. At that time, however, I subordinated it to scuba diving, because it was too soon after graduation from university to commit myself to two expensive hobbies. While the idea of such a licence has somehow faded away over the last years, it never disappeared entirely. Therefore, it is no surprise that it re-enters the stage now that I am looking for more hobbies and scuba diving has made it into a less expensive phase, as I have not only left the bulk of expenditures for courses and equipment behind, but can also generate some extra cash by teaching courses. I am certainly not going to subordinate scuba diving to such a new hobby, but photography and steering small planes appear to make an exciting and fulfilling mix with scuba diving.

After all, even this book can be seen as a direct result of my time abroad and an example of taking my life into my own hands. Several years ago I drafted a bucket list with things which I want to do or achieve in my life. Writing and publishing a book was one of them. Whereas the list became very short or even almost entirely erased within a surprisingly short period of time, as I had on one hand highly underestimated my capability of achieving things and on the other hand started shifting my goals away from materialistic possessions, my ambition to write and publish a book stayed despite becoming well hidden somewhere in my unconscious mind. I was simply lacking the inspiration to come up with something to write about. Therefore, I am still surprised and amazed, when I now realize my progress on a long-held dream, which I did not think I would ever achieve and I would probably not have realized without the experiences of the last twelve months. It impresses me even more to realize that I did not plan for it, but spontaneously started typing during one of the most inspiring periods of my life. Hence, my work on this book has become one of the most tangible evidences for how great things will happen if we approach our life proactively, do not fear to step out of our comfort zone and maintain an open mind to let things happen.

The time, by when I started to write this book, does emphasize again the importance of proactively seeking experiences and inspirations for our life. As already expressed, I have been ambitious to write my own book for a long time, but only found the inspiration to do so when breaking loose from my mediocre life one year ago. In fact, I had already come to understand the discussed principles and paradigms from studying some of the world's best-selling books over the previous years, but only got to experience their true meaning now, as they unveiled their full potential when being applied to my journey. This need for experiences and inspirations becomes even more apparent now that I am back in Germany, living in the same apartment as one year ago. While I always felt a flush of inspiration as soon as I started to work on this book in Thailand and usually recognized it as a way to remind myself about the greatness of my life, things started to change when flying to Stockholm in March. I was still eager to finish my work and always felt great soon after starting to type, but could easily notice that it was getting more difficult to get into the flow of writing with the same pace as external inspirations were fading away. It was, nevertheless, still somehow easy to find the muse to continue the work, as I continued living a somewhat extraordinary life. However, since my return to Germany three weeks ago and even more since starting my new job a week ago it starts feeling more like a task than like a passion. It is a bit sad to realize that this book is becoming a smaller part of me being and a bigger part of me doing. It, however, remains a good reminder for me not to allow myself to go back into my old mindset.

As I am now eager to continue writing in the future and even see this as an option for the time after retirement at some point, it becomes self-evident how important it is that I remain proactive in pushing to keep my life exciting and inspirational. It, therefore, fills me with satisfaction that as another side effect this journey has grown my entrepreneurial spirit to some extent. My learnt lessons in terms of accepting uncertainty and risk, making my life lean and taking ownership of my life – only to mention a few – have triggered my mindset to develop into an interesting direction. I have always been impressed by the ability of some of the most famous entrepreneurs to build something great from scratch, but never found the inspiration to do so myself. Having experienced now in a highly impressive way the power of small decisions and steps to make great change, my readiness to be entrepreneurial on a small scale has certainly increased. While this book is probably one of the most tangible outcomes of this awakened spirit so far, I feel a strong desire to work on some of my new ideas for small online businesses and how to earn some extra money online. It is only my reflections discussed in section 4.2 which is holding me back from doing so right now, as I do not want to repeat my past mistake of starting too many projects at the same time. That would result in falling back into living less mindfully, appreciating less what I am doing and, consequently, spending my life doing instead of being. Nevertheless, time for these projects will come as soon as this book requires less attention, when I progress from the deep work of writing to the more practical work of selling it. There is a very thin line between making active use of our time on one hand and packing our life too much on the other. I have come back from Thailand so highly inspired and full of ideas that I now need to be careful not to sacrifice every space and flexibility in my life for a false sense of productivity. As a mentor of mine once said in reflection of my life: "Piling twice as much on your plate does not take you anywhere. It is digesting your food that brings you growth". My time in Ibiza and Thailand has certainly provided a great experience of piling less and digesting more, consequently growing more.

I am almost certainly not going to be a great entrepreneur with my own flourishing business, but these experiences and insights of the last twelve months have triggered a development and spirit in me, which will certainly have a positive impact on my life. After all, while not everyone can earn money from being an entrepreneur, we all have an entrepreneurial responsibility for living our life. In contrast to our daily work as an employee of some company, in life we cannot rely on a supervisor to guide us into any direction. We need to take the driver's seat of life ourselves. One of my main learnings comes from the insight that our level of risk affinity is one of the most significant determinants for how much life we add into the years which are available to us. The willingness to accept risk and readiness to fail is what many of the great entrepreneurs have in common. It is impressive to realize how positive the impact of my own risk acceptance on my life during the last twelve months has been and how different my life would have been and would still be if I had placed too much value on certainty and predictability.

As I have elaborated before, my return to Europe happened entirely different than planned. Instead of taking a flight from Singapore to Frankfurt by the end of March, the escalating COVID-19 pandemic at that point changed my plans and made me take a flight from Bangkok to Stockholm, so I could spend time with my girlfriend before lockdowns in further countries made that impossible for an unforeseeable time. While this decision appeared wise from an emotional perspective, my rationale mind was as alert as never before that this was as wrong a decision as it could be at a time when governments around the globe were calling upon their citizens abroad to return home as soon as possible. My family got highly anxious that I was going to jeopardize my new job, which I was supposed to start by the 1st of May. I cannot deny that going to Stockholm at a time, when Germany was on the edge of a nationwide lockdown and nobody could foresee what would happen next, placed a significant amount of risk into my life. My rationale for going despite these uncertainties was simple and twofold.

Firstly, nobody was able to anticipate at all what Europe and the world would look like seven weeks later, when I was supposed to start my new job. Therefore, it appeared entirely irrational to take this unpredictable future into account and give up every positive aspect of life in an attempt to eliminate every potential risk, much of which was even perceived only rather than an actual threat. I am in the process of making it a habit and principle of mine to consider the most critical foreseeable impacts, but not let those, which cannot be anticipated, hold me back from taking decisions and, consequently, force me into mediocracy. If I would not have been able to make it home in time for my job, adherence to the agreed upon start date would have been one of the least concerns in a bigger context for my new employer and me. Secondly, the main risks from not returning to Germany right away were the potential unavailability of flight connections between Stockholm and Germany and an eventually imposed stay home notice and obligatory quarantine upon entering the country. When I am now reflecting on the last weeks, I am happy that I did not resign to my risk aversion but accepted to keep things open. After all, the worst-case scenario would have been a challenging and somehow adventurous travel to Germany and a 14 days quarantine before starting my new job. Fortunately, only the latter became true, as a minimum flight schedule remained uphold between major European cities. While I could have easily avoided the quarantine as well, if I had simply returned home earlier, it appeared as a reasonable cost to pay. With no doubt, spending five weeks with my girlfriend in a country without heavy restrictions on public life plus two weeks of locked into my apartment was a much better choice than not seeing my girlfriend and spending seven weeks in a country with not much to do due to an ongoing lockdown.

As I am now at a critical point, at which I need to determine whether I fall back into a mediocre life or further nourish my proactive mindset, which has grown so much over the last twelve months, it appears more important than ever to keep the memories of this exciting time alive and remind myself and my readers of the main learnings and insights in this context. As this chapter is called "Take Full Ownership of Your Life & Don't Be Afraid to Take Risks", it is no surprise that the main learnings relate to how significantly these two paradigms can influence our life, as my last twelve months have shown in one of the most extraordinary and powerful ways. To prevent mediocracy and live a fulfilled and memorable life instead, we must never wait for things to happen but be proactive in filling our life with excitement and inspirations, which will provide us food for growth. Sometimes this requires making sacrifices and accepting a certain level of risk. Therefore, it is important to never allow ourselves to subordinate all kinds of adventures and excitement to a false sense of security, as long as we keep a certain safety net in place. We need to accept the possibility to fail, as we would otherwise accept to miss out on great opportunities for growth. This often requires us to make our decisions based on a limited set of information, as we will never be able to foresee all potential consequences. The worst decision we can take is, however, to procrastinate a decision in the first place.

Once we do not allow our risk aversion to hold us back from trying out new things and stepping outside our comfort zone regularly, we face a great opportunity to live our life to the fullest. However, overcoming our risk aversion is only one critical step in the process of taking full ownership of our life. Furthermore, we must learn to let go of our habit to use our circumstances and perceived social expectations as an excuse. In the end, we have our life to live and must, therefore, listen to our own desires much more than placing too much importance on what others think how we should live our life. After all, we can heavily enrich our understanding if we listen to and consider other people's perspective, but we shall not take it as the only truth, to which we subordinate our beliefs and desires. Replacing our deeply embedded reactive "If only I could…" paradigm by the much more proactive "I will… no matter what it takes" approach is already a simple but highly powerful first step. Nevertheless, we must then be careful to not squeeze too much into our life, as we need to keep the flexibility and room for our proactivity to unfold its beautiful impacts.

I am not claiming that I am the first one to write about these principles, as they have already been discussed and I have already understood them long before my time in Ibiza and Koh Tao. It is, however, impressive and intriguing to realize that it took me to step out of my comfort zone and well-established life for twelve months to make them surface from my unconscious and abstract knowledge to fully unfold their beautiful impact in practical ways. Having to build a new life from scratch and allowing for slack in my schedule because of letting go of perceived responsibilities has certainly turned out as one of the most valuable experiences of this incredibly special year. While I now need to be careful to not cut my wings and grow my roots again, I would certainly be a significantly less mature and proactive person now if I had not followed my dream and gone on this exciting journey. Typing these lines powerfully brings back those memories, which are now so important in nourishing my willingness to live a proactive life. After all, we have one life to live and the last thing I want is to end up in regret about letting go of my dreams and missing out on great opportunities. I have now lived my dream for one year, but need to make sure that the journey does not stop here.

4.5 Being Introvert in an Extrovert Life

Every episode in life comes with new challenges. Living the life of a scuba diving instructor, who is constantly surrounded by happy people in holiday mood and sup-posed to spread a positive atmosphere, is obviously hugely different from that of a project manager, who spends a significant deal of hours in a neon-lit office. When I am now reflecting on this period between May 2019 and March 2020, this change turned out as one of the greatest challenges for me. When we want to learn more about ourselves and browse the internet for input, we come across a lot of personality type tests, which classify people along linear scales in more or fewer dimensions. A common spectrum across many of these tests relates to where we get our energy from. On one end of the scale we can find the more introvert personalities. While they need calmness and "Me Time" to recharge their inner batteries and process information, the more extrovert characters on the other end are quite the opposite. They recharge their batteries and process information in more social settings while talking their thoughts through with their peers. None of these preferences is generally better than the other. However, every job has certain characteristics, which fit better into one of these personality types, as it depends on our preferences which kind of situation acts as a stressor for us.

After reading the header for this chapter and the subsequent opening lines it should come as no surprise that I find myself on the more introvert end of the scale. While this preference has nothing to do with how we see people, my lifestyle of the last years has certainly been impacted by it a lot. As it is quite typical for the introvert personalities, I usually preferred having a few deep relations rather than being with many people and constantly getting to know more. After stressful days at work with a lot of phone calls, discussions and interactions I usually felt a longing for being on my own, either doing workout or simply relaxing at home. Using the evenings for socializing with other people usually appeared appealing after days with less interactions. In other words, when there was no need to recharge the inner batteries of the introvert me.

The common stereotype of scuba diving instructors is quite different. Despite not having done any empiric research, I dare to say that extroversion is a wide-spread trait among people doing this job and living the associated lifestyle. Whenever I went on a scuba diving vacation during the last years, I was impressed by the laid-back and easy-going personalities of the instructors and dive masters, who I got to know. I usually admired how easy it was for them to approach people and how natural they appeared in engaging with new customers in social settings every day. As I had been surrounded by pretty much the same people for a long time and had not gotten to know a big number of new people, those guys were living the life I dreamt of and which I was ambitious to achieve when going abroad as a scuba diving instructor myself. I saw a vision of myself more easily interacting with others and, consequently, living a more social life. Obviously, I met and got to know a lot of interesting and open-minded people during my journey. However, I had to learn that living this lifestyle does not take away my responsibility for being proactive in interacting and engaging with them. Furthermore, I anticipated in no way how big a stressor for an introvert person it can become to constantly meet new people and deal with little privacy in my free time.

It was one aspect of my life in Ibiza that turned out as a great stressor for the introvert part of my personality. It is a common practice across dive centres that free accommodation is included in the remuneration package for their dive masters and instructors. My dive centre in Ibiza was no exception in this regard. However, it was on the more extreme side, as my colleagues and I had our rooms inside the dive centre, my room even having its window into the busy beach and into the public area of the dive centre, where our guests tended to socialize with our managers and staff after their dives. It is easy to guess that there was little to no privacy to find at my accommodation and that the only way to get some was to go for extended walks along the beautiful beaches of the island. When I was planning my year off, I had a vision of an easy and relaxed life on the beach, while being surrounded by interesting and happy people. To some extent, I got this expectation accomplished. A longing to take a break from this lifestyle and escape to our own private area every now and then is, however, probably just human, and self-evident for the more introvert people. Therefore, as much fun life was at times, it was stressing every sense of joy and appreciation out of me at others, especially when the exhaustion from a long day or week of work was coming down on me or certain things were not going as desired.

While the reader might now suspect that this experience fills me with regret for some of my choices, I am instead full of appreciation for the challenge and learning it provided. It is usually the challenging and harder periods of our life, in which we get to know ourselves better and, consequently, grow as a person. When I am now reflecting on these twelve months of my life, living an extrovert lifestyle as an introvert person turned out as the most underestimated challenge on one hand, but as the most valuable and powerful trigger for insights and learnings on the other. Looking at my learnings with a more abstract perspective now, I can categorize them into four distinct areas. Two of them are more practical, as they relate to making more conscious use of the few quiet moments, we have on one hand and being more social while hiding our internal sense of stress on the other. The other two learnings go deeper into our fundamental paradigms and relate to the discussions from two of the previous chapters of this book, as they shed additional light on our unlimited responsibility for how our life goes and the necessity to decide to be happy instead of blaming our lack of happiness on our external circumstances. I will go through these four areas and discuss them in detail one by one throughout the next pages.

Let us start with some thoughts on making more conscious use of the few quiet moments we have. Working and living at a busy dive centre during peak season leaves no quiet moments during business hours. There was no way that I could hide and spent some time inwards-focused, as customers expected their questions to be answered or simply wanted to socialize with their instructor. Let us face it... Most of my customers was having a good time, being on a well-deserved vacation for a few weeks and, fortunately and for a good reason, excited about learning to dive, for some of them a dream they had held for a long time. While there was absolutely nothing wrong with that and I had probably been the same on many of my diving vacations before, for some of them it came with a lack of understanding that my colleagues and I were not on vacation. However, as I had chosen to live this life out of my own free will, there was no way I was not going to embody the image which people tend to have of scuba diving instructors. It was self-evident for me that everything I did and said had to transmit the clear message that scuba diving is fun. Consequently, being underwater and not being able to talk often turned out as rare and adorable moments to satisfy the introvert part of my personality. So far so good... Everyone's life and work come with exhausting and stressful moments. However, what made my time the challenge and valuable experience was the fact that the extrovert lifestyle and lack of privacy was not limited to work hours but continued in the evenings and weekends. The level of shatter around me remained on a constantly high level even in times which were supposed to be relaxing.

Whereas I had lived a highly introvert life until April 2019, spending a big portion of my free time at home without even being fully aware that this more or less conscious decision resulted from one specific part of my personality, I could suddenly hardly find the quiet moments and peace, which my brain so desperately needed to relax. It turned out as a long needed and highly valuable lesson in mindfulness. Instead of reactively and passively wasting my evenings on the sofa, with some fuzzy awareness about the cause for my lack of desire to go out and do things, I was now forced to proactively seek moments of conscious "Me Time" by leaving the scene and taking the time I needed to recharge to come back a bit later and take part in life as it was going on in the dive centre's social area. Therefore, I learnt in a powerful way the importance of making use of the little quiet moments and adore them instead of simply substituting the reduced activity around me with digital distractions and shatter from my smartphone. After all, it took a change of perspective to refresh my awareness that calming down the mind is not only possible on the sofa or doing exhausting exercise like running but also enjoying the little things of life, as for example a walk along the beach, a swim in the ocean or simply sunbathing and reading a good book.

The abovementioned need to find quiet locations instead of simply hiding at home triggered another interesting experience and learning for the introvert me. It appears as a common trait for the more introvert personalities to avoid attention of any kind and not stand out of the crowd. In previous years, this characteristic has usually most visibly shown itself when we were playing charade as a party game. While many of my more extrovert friends obviously enjoyed a lot to make an as big as possible fool out of themselves, I was usually nervously waiting for the moment for me to go on stage, as I hated standing in the spotlight and acting like a fool. The feedback of a colleague of mine in Ibiza to simply do what I want and not care about what others think came as a very exact summary of what has been holding me back from many things in my life so far. It even begins with the ridiculously small things such as leaving the dive centre and going for a walk, when everyone else was sitting together and sharing their stories over one or more beers. Obviously, there was always someone who raised the question why I was not joining them, and it is exactly this perceived need for justification that way too often lets the introverts blend in instead of doing what they really desire. However, a simple "I need some time for myself" almost always sufficed as an effective and accepted answer and was nothing to be scared or feel wrong about. And let us face it... Those people who do not accept it, and I certainly met these people as well, are most likely not worth bothering about much anyways.

Earlier in this book I have already reflected a bit on how I expect my year as a scuba diving instructor to impact my career outside scuba diving. While many people believe that it does not at all go in line with a corporate career, I have experienced and am convinced that it can in fact have a significant positive impact. I have already elaborated how easy it was to find a well-paid job after Thailand without placing a single application. It should, therefore, be evident by now that I have not experienced any setback on my career. In fact, I am convinced that many of the experiences and personality improvements will benefit my life and career in the long-term. One of them relates to being an introvert in an extrovert life. As I was supposed to and wanted to be the happy and sympathetic instructor during the day and did not want to excessively hide from socializing in the evenings either, it becomes evident that I had moments, when I felt some tension or stress inside with no chance to release it. Instead, I wanted to be the social and easy-going guy and so I had to hide what was going on inside me. It turned out as a challenge, as I usually tend to unintendedly show my emotions. However, in everyone's life and career certain situations are better handled when looking at our emotions from an abstract perspective and seeing them as what they are instead of giving in letting them control our behaviour. The latter way too often leads to unnecessary and undesired conflict. Therefore, time will have to show in how far my life and career in the long-term will benefit from constantly being surrounded by people for an extended period. I am, however, convinced that it will benefit me a lot by having provided me a lesson in not letting emotions or other sorts of feelings steer my behaviour, a lesson which I had successfully been hiding from for several years.

More understanding and empathy for instructors and divemasters, when I will go on diving vacations myself again, is certainly one of the things I am taking away from this period of my life. I had the opportunity to experience the joy of being a scuba diving instructor, but I also learnt to acknowledge how sometimes the constant need to be happy and social can lead to stress and tension. As everything in life comes with certain challenges, this experience will not hold me back from breaking loose from the rat race again at some point in my life. It is valuable to keep in mind, however, to have clear and realistic expectations. It is interesting how this experience of living an extrovert life as an introvert enables a synthesis of the different learnings discussed in this book, as it relates strongly to three of the other sections of this chapter.

Firstly, feeling stressed by what I had desired for several years, turned out as a highly impressive manifestation of section 4.3 "Happiness Will Not Find You". As already elaborated, I had lived a very introvert life until April 2019. Instead of going out and meeting new people a lot, I held on to a few selected deeper relations. While there was objectively nothing wrong with that and I was not taking any sincere and effective action to meet new people, I always envied the outgoing and social attitude of many scuba diving instructors around the world and was dreaming of living this life myself. Taking an honest look, this aspect appears as a significant part of my motivation to embark on this one-year adventure. Luckily, I got this ambition fully accomplished in Ibiza and Thailand. I got to know new people daily, some of which turned out as friends, who I am still in contact with. However, instead of appreciating this new lifestyle as much as possible, the sudden lack of privacy made me feel a strong desire to spend time on my own again. I finally got what I had desired but started missing what I had been used to before. One can imagine how great it felt when the peak season in Ibiza was drawing to its close and I could spend some quiet evenings watching a movie in my room instead of socializing and having drinks with guests. The whole dilemma became visible again during and after my transition to Koh Tao. As I had no dive centre arrange accommodation for me, I had to rent a place myself and it naturally came with more privacy than a room next to the dive centre's office. Unsurprisingly, I appreciated this progress a lot at first, as it provided exactly what I had been missing so much in Ibiza. However, as discussed before, I never utilized this newly gained privacy, as I was too afraid of missing life as it was going on elsewhere on the island. I finally possessed what I missed in Ibiza but never appreciated or made use of it. The loop was now complete. Leaving Germany, I had left my introvert life full of a longing for extroversion behind and started living an extrovert life in Ibiza, full of a longing for satisfying the introvert me better. Moving to Thailand I had left the forced extrovert life of Ibiza behind and finally got what I had missed but started to live an extrovert life out of my own free will. While it illustrates the positive impact which my sabbatical has had on me, as it shows my greater focus on a social life, it also points out again how much joy and happiness gets lost in focussing on what we do not have instead of appreciating what we have.

It is also worth reflecting on the depth and width of the relations you typically make as a scuba diving instructor. As I already indicated a few lines ago, I used to live by common introvert preferences, as before my year off I used to have a few deeper relations instead of many shallow ones. One can imagine that things are quite different as a scuba diving instructor. As expected, I met and got to know new people daily, but it was self-evident from the first moment that despite a deeper connection with a few of them, I would see them for a few days or maximum weeks but then not again.

Obviously, there were also fellow instructors and divemasters at the dive centres, who were supposed to stay longer, and a certain level of friendship developed with some of them. However, there was also a hitch in these relations. As I was only planning this period of my life for a limited number of months, it turned out difficult for me to see the long-term perspective in these friendships. As inspiring and fun it can be to constantly get in and out of encounters with a lot of interesting people from all over the world, as challenging it turned out for me that the fundamental setup condemned these relations to stay relatively shallow right from the beginning. In section 4.2 "Spend Your Life Being Instead of Doing" I discussed the importance of simply being and living your life instead of constantly optimizing your time and doing everything with a certain purpose or goal in mind. This direly needed lesson emphasizes my need to change a paradigm, which now also appears to be part of the cause for my struggle with having a lot of width instead of depth in my relations. I sometimes struggled to invest energy and time into getting to know the people around me, as part of my personality kept on insisting in my unconscious mind that the return on these investments would not last long and be limited to a few days only. Now that I am looking back, however, it is worth reflecting on the question why there needs to be a long-lasting return on all our social efforts, while we can also simply enjoy listening to newly met people and seeing the world from their perspective.

I do not want to be misunderstood here. I am certainly not populating the idea that deep relations are not important. In fact, I am not even advertising that many shallow relations are more important than a few deeper ones. I am still convinced, in fact more than ever, that investing in and committing to deep and meaningful relations over a long time is one way to find and nourish meaning in our life. However, there is no decision to be made between depth and width. There is no single deep relation to be given up for the sake of getting to know a lot of people. When I am looking back in all honesty now, I did not sacrifice a single deep relation for the sake of going abroad and meeting a lot of new people. In fact, I can now conclude for the closest of my friends that I did not even see them less during this year than before, as I have never been used to seeing them more often than every six months or so anyways. After all, closeness does not require seeing each other often, but is so much more about having a deep connection of some kind. And that is how it can become a highly enriching addition to our life, if we sincerely listen to the stories and perspectives of the people around us, for the simple sake of being with them without any long-term purpose or return on investment in mind. While our long-invested deep relations provide us an anchor and stable fundamentals, we can get many new inspirations to keep us thriving from the many people we meet along the way. While the people close to us have by now likely earned the trust required to challenge our way of thinking and provide us highly valuable second thoughts, we might know them too well to find entirely new inspirations. Having lived with the same partner for a long time, it is even possible that we have developed mutual habits as well as similar ways of seeing the world and living our life. This is where meeting new people unfolds its true potential, as it enables us to look at the world and our life from an entirely new perspective. Sustainable personal growth can originate from the synthesis of inspiring acquaintances and challenging long-term relations. However, we must be open for the benefits of and ready to invest in both. We must be ready to simply be with people instead of questioning every encounter for its long-term potential.

Having so far elaborated on making use of the few quiet moments we got, deciding to appreciate what we have in our life and getting inspired from the people we meet, it is time to look at what this year has taught me about my own role in how many people I meet. While above I have reflected on the value of being open and curious in all encounters with people despite not always seeing potential for a long-term relation, this whole discussion becomes obsolete without enough conscious effort to actively meet people. Section 4.4 "Take Full Ownership of Your Life & Don't Be Afraid to Take Risks" was all about not blaming our environment for how our life goes but instead identifying what we really want and then doing it no matter what. One of the main drivers behind my decision to become a scuba diving instructor was my ambition to meet more people than in my previous life and, let us be all honest, also those of the opposite sex. Life and work as scuba diving instructor held its promise in so far that I did indeed meet new people daily. However, it has also taught me an important lesson. Living an extroverted life and being thrown into encounters with new people daily does not automatically lead to getting to know them. It is still our own unlimited responsibility to indulge in these encounters and make them unfold their full potential.

It is psychologically a lot easier to blame external factors for what is going wrong in our life than to accept that we ourselves are the only ones to blame. Unfortunately, I had lived by this faulty and dangerous paradigm for too long, always blaming my failure in getting to know people on living in the wrong place, having too many other things to take care of and all the other common excuses. While one might now argue that even these conditions can be changed, if we really want, it was always just too easy to bring these excuses forward. It did not take me until April 2019 to acknowledge them as simple excuses. My year in Ibiza and Thailand, however, uncovered the ugly truth to an extent that I could not deny it any longer. I had finally eliminated those aspects of my life which I used to blame for my limited social activity, but I had to learn that it does not take away the need for proactiveness in order to be socially successful. It came as an intriguing insight that despite having the right circumstances there is no guarantee for connecting with the people around us. Living an extroverted lifestyle does not automatically make us successful and guarantee us friends, if our mindset and behaviour do not change.

Being surrounded by many people does not necessarily lead to interacting with them. It is important to understand that we are not the only ones who are surrounded by a lot of people. Also, the people who we are eager to engage with have a variety of people to choose from. Therefore, it was an interesting experience that we are in no way special or standing out of the crowd. It does in the end not make any difference whether we are surrounded by few or many people. An incredibly huge number of divemasters and instructors is living on Koh Tao, so that even being one of them did not guarantee the attention of other people. I still had to be active in starting interaction with them. It was, however, a positive side effect of having left my bubble and comfort zone behind that I felt a strong desire to get to know people. While in my previous life it was easy to hide behind my well-established routines, it suddenly would have felt like a wasted opportunity if I did not actively approach people during these few months. Thus, I worked up the courage to actively approach more people than ever before in my life and the reactions were almost always positive.

The common stereotype associated with living a scuba diving instructor's life, and that of many similar jobs alike, turned out as only partially true. Being in this role, does not necessarily make you the centre of attention and guarantee you a lot of friends and sexual relations. I experienced an incredibly huge potential arising from living in a sunny place and being surrounded by happy and open-minded people all the time. On the other hand, however, I also learnt that nothing except for job and location will change, if our mindset and behaviour do not change. Leaving the bubble of my old life has emphasized again the need for proactiveness, as living in an easy-going surrounding did not automatically make me easy-going as well. Despite all the outgoing people around me, my personality preference for introversion still prevailed, so that it required a conscious effort to blend into this new lifestyle. However, as I had decided to live as a scuba diving instructor to challenge my thinking, I accepted the challenge and was rewarded with a lot of small successes and personal developments for the better. Hence, leaving my bubble and taking a leap out of my comfort zone has once again proven to be an incredibly important and powerful means to make progress as a person and fill our life with joy.

It was one of the more obvious and rewarding personal developments to become more at ease approaching people and leading small talk. So far having lived my life with a strong introvert preference and my previously discussed focus on doing things rather than simply being, I have always struggled a lot to approach people for the sole purpose of getting to know them as well as to be the conversation starter in social settings. While it has usually never been difficult to approach people with confidence if there was a specific reason to do so, I have always struggled, and still do, to initiate small talk. The ability to initiate small talk, however, plays a key role in how socially successful we are and how many people we get to know. I am, therefore, happy that my sabbatical has also challenged and provided me valuable insights in this area and brought to my conscious awareness how big an impact our personality and preferences have on our life. As soon as I stepped on Spanish ground in Ibiza, I could no longer hide behind my routines and my illusion that everything would be better anyways as soon as I have become a scuba diving instructor. Finally, I had to act and accept responsibility for how my life goes if I wanted to avoid losing the opportunity of a year full of potential. So, I set myself an improvement goal and took conscious steps to achieve it.

The challenge, which I set for myself, was simple but powerful. Up until 2019 I had been used to only approaching people if there was a specific reason to do so. It did not matter whether it was for asking for directions, requesting the help of a shop clerk or asking the bus driver for directions. If there was a perceived legitimation to talk to someone, it was easy to do so with confidence and without hesitation. Approaching people for the sole sake of starting a conversation, however, usually turned out as a great obstacle that led to procrastination until the opportunity was gone. Therefore, I set myself a goal during certain periods in Ibiza and Koh Tao to initiate small talk with at least one random person a day. It became much easier, when I acknowledged that it does not require any creative opening line but can be as simple as asking for the time. It still took a big effort to shut down that inner voice, which insisted on questioning the chance for any meaningful outcomes of these conversations and continued reminding me that people might not want to talk and react differently than desired. This paradigm is highly dangerous though. Every initiative and every interaction led to some positive outcome, even if it were only to improve my self-confidence through seeing the open and positive reaction which I received in most of my attempts. But let us face it... We all have probably had some seemingly meaningless moments in life, which unexpectedly led to some great developments, some of which had the potential for changing our life forever. It is, therefore, essential to acknowledge and be open for the tiny chance for surprising developments and not ignore them under the presence of the overwhelming probability that we will go through just one more meaningless interaction. After all, there is nothing to lose. If we have a short conversation and then wander away or even if we receive a rejection, we will not be worse off than before if we take the rejection as what it is. There is no reason to let a rejection lower our self-esteem. The other person can have a variety of reasons not to want to talk to us, having had a bad day or being in a hurry just to mention a few, but it is hardly ever a judgement of us as a person. Once I had overcome these doubts, it became much easier to initiate small talk with random people and it felt great, as the interactions were extending beyond asking for the time and turned into actual conversations for a couple of minutes. When I now look back, I am convinced that this development would not have happened, if I had stayed within my comfort zone of my old life. Leaving my routines behind has once again led to some moments of high nervosity at first, but great growth and satisfaction once I had overcome the fear and left my bubble behind.

In conclusion, being thrown into an extroverted life turned out as maybe the most underestimated challenge of my entire adventure. My dream of living such a life has always been my most important motivator to embark on this adventure, but I have never anticipated it to be such an important stressor and eye-opening experience. I had always envisioned this lifestyle to be great and I can say now that this expectation has been met. However, it was intriguing to realize that for beauty to unfold it is not enough to change your environment. It is way more important to change your mindset and that is possible independent from whether you break loose from your life or not.

Thus, my time abroad has not only turned out as a break and a great time, but also as a trim tab towards a more fulfilling future. If I had not taken the proactive step out of my self-imposed bubble, I would have continued hiding behind the few relations I had and would have never acknowledged the need to go out and meet new people as powerfully as I did in Ibiza and Thailand. Once I had removed all the excuses and distractions in my well-established life, I could no longer refuse to take an honest look at my situation.

As usual, this honest look hurt at first. It is never easy to acknowledge the opportunities which we missed in our life so far. It was not easy to accept that the faults of my previous life and the missed opportunities for living life to its fullest were in no way due to my circumstances but purely due to the introvert decisions I took. Even though I had been somehow aware of this fact before, I had to go off the beaten track and look at my life from a different perspective to fully acknowledge what was going on. As painful and difficult these changes of perspective usually are as valuable and important are they at the same time. If I had not gone this path through Ibiza and Koh Tao, I would have continued living my introvert life while admiring those people who live the life I want. I would not have learned in such a powerful way that changing our environment without changing our mindset and behaviour takes us nowhere. Meeting interesting people from all around the world does not automatically provide us joy, if we do not actively and consciously decide to put effort into engaging with them and openly listening to their stories and experiences. It has turned out as a very challenging, but at the same time very inspiring, experience to be thrown into an extrovert lifestyle as an introvert person. It has once again signified the importance of continuously challenging our habits and changing those which do not provide the desired outcomes, while it is psychologically so much easier to continue them and make up excuses and blame external factors for not achieving what we want to achieve. Challenging and changing long-kept habits is never easy, but it is possible and necessary, if they are not leading us to where we want to be. I have experienced first-hand that even drastic changes like quitting a job and moving to Spain or Thailand to live and work as a scuba diving instructor is still no guarantee for achieving what we hope to achieve. It provides a promising environment, but then it is still our daily decisions and actions which determine how our life goes.

Whereas it has become such a powerful and valuable lesson to live an extroverted lifestyle for eleven months, it is now my main challenge to take these learnings forward, not allow the spirit to fade away and take proactive and sincere effort to change my habits and live a more active life. I am writing these lines from home four months after returning from Thailand and can already realize how I am slowly getting sucked back into my old habits and routines. It is, therefore, important to put a conscious and proactive effort into keeping my habits from Ibiza and Koh Tao alive. Even if a strong preference for introversion prevails, it is possible to push for more balance between extroversion and introversion. As I have already elaborated earlier in this book, comfort zones expand with every step we take outside their boundaries. It is, therefore, also possible to challenge ourselves to live outside the boundaries of our comfortable introvert lifestyle and we will notice how the boundaries will start to move. Step by step we will feel more comfortable living a more active lifestyle with more social interactions, which does of course not mean that we need to deny our original preferences. Our preferences will prevail as a save harbour to return to if needed, but more possibilities will emerge for life to unfold.

September 2012 has been one of the most ambitious and inspiring periods of my life. The opportunities and dreams were endless, as I had just graduated from university and was looking forward to a successful career. I was at the point where seven years at university had been meant to take me and I envisioned myself wearing a fashionable suit, driving a glamorous car and taking clients out for fancy business dinners while successfully climbing the career ladder. Seven years later I find myself wearing swim shorts and a partly ripped rash guard, driving a motorbike in disputable conditions and joining backpacking students for cheap Pad Thai and beer for dinner at restaurants which look as if the next strong wind will blow them away. What may at first sound like a failed career and broken existence, was after all a conscious decision and necessary realignment with my most inner values. It is, however, worth the reflection how this side-track and adventure has jeopardized the mission which I have set out for my life.

It does not appear as a too hypothetical assumption that most people have or seek a mission of some kind for their life. Some strive for making a great career and becoming the CEO of their company, others want to be the best parents they can be for their kids and some aim for nothing less than making the world a better place. As I do not want to be misunderstood, and this last sentence can easily sound ironical, I want it to be clear that I consider each of these valid and realistic goals, if we do not make our entire self-esteem dependent on their accomplishment and have a realistic view of our chances. Even the third one appears legit, as making the world a better place starts with the tiniest contributions. While I certainly also have goals in mind for my life, I have chosen a different approach for my mission. Inspired by one of my favourite authors I have composed a very personal mission statement for my life several years ago. I have put on paper what matters most for me and should therefore guide my daily decisions and behaviour. It does not contain goals, which can be considered achieved at some point. Instead, it contains timeless principles that reflect my most inner values, such fundamental things as supporting my family, being mindful in whatever I do and not being afraid of giving more than I take. As such, my mission statement acts as a red line and guiding force amidst all the turbulences that life inevitably sometimes confronts us with.

Quitting my job, packing my stuff, and boarding a one-way flight to Ibiza has certainly been one of the greatest turbulences within the last years. This decision unavoidably raised the question, and some of my friends asked it frankly, if it was a good decision to give up everything I achieved so far and put in danger what I still wanted to achieve in my life. Those who read on will learn that I have lost none of the things which made my previous life worthwhile and have instead gained so many things which are enriching my life now. But we shall start with a short reflection of which values from my mission statement were put into jeopardy and which ones benefited from taking a leap out of my forward lifestyle.

It would be naïve to believe that I would not have to neglect any of my values, when living this life for eleven months. After all, my mission statement contains such things as focusing on healthy food, drinking little to no alcohol, and exercising at least four times a week. While I lived up to them quite successfully until April 2019, I let go almost completely thereafter. Alcohol became a regular companion when socializing after the day's diving, I did not do any sports besides diving at all in Thailand, and during the busiest peak times in Ibiza lunch often meant stuffing in whatever I found for the pure sake of not starving. After Thailand I returned home with six kilograms more than before, but it seemed acceptable, as it was meant to be a temporary endeavour. Fortunately, these negative impacts were only temporary, as I managed to re-align with my values soon after returning to Europe and it did not take long to lose the six kilograms and even more, as Ibiza and Thailand had made me used to eating less sweets. Consequently, my lifestyle became healthier than ever once I cut down on the alcohol. Therefore, my mission statement has succeeded to allow for turbulences and side-tracks while keeping my true values in mind and bringing me back on track when the time had come.

It comes with great satisfaction, however, that these months positively influenced many of my values. Living life, following my passion, and proactively connecting with other people are some of the more obvious ones, which benefited a lot after having been neglected for a long time. In some way or another, the developments described in the previous chapter relate to long neglected values and beliefs of mine. Some other impacts came as a surprise, but are satisfying me even more, as they are persisting now after having returned home a few months ago. My improved relationship with my family is probably one of the least expected outcomes. It comes easy to suspect that it would suffer from being disconnected for a year. However, after living close to my parents for almost my entire life, living more than 10,000 km away transformed our relationship from quantity to quality. The quality of our conversations improved a lot, once we were geographically disconnected and had more things to discuss. This improved relationship with my family appears to be partly a result of becoming more independent mentally. As I broke loose from the conservative social norms of my hometown and surrounded myself with more alternatively thinking minds, I started to be more comfortable to share my ideas and thoughts without being afraid of what others would think about them. Before this transitional experience, I would have hesitated a lot to let others know that I am writing this book, afraid of appearing as an illusional dreamer. Now it feels natural to tell others and the reactions are always positive.

So, I can conclude that my sabbatical has in no way jeopardized my life's mission, as the negative impacts were only temporary, while the positive ones are lasting. After all, I do not realize any negative impacts on my career, family, or friends that matter, but a drastically improved mental well-being in the sense of feeling impressively more connected with my values and centred in my life. In fact, my sense of having a mission and meaning in my life has grown stronger than ever. Over the last years my motivation and sense of direction emerged mainly from my goal to become a scuba diving instructor and work as such, while my long-term vision for the time thereafter was quite limited. As I already elaborated a bit earlier in this book, the accomplishment of this goal made me struggle for a while, since it meant that my main motivational driver was gone. It was this psychological vacuum together with the drastic change in my environment, however, which helped me gain clarity on my values, passions and long-term vision.

My career was going reasonably successful during the last years. However, it only served as a reliable source of income, but made me obliged to get up in the morning instead of wanting to, as it did in no way tab into my passion. While this grew into a significant source of frustration, I struggled to pinpoint which changes to my career would lead to more job satisfaction. Taking a year off and finding the muse to indulge into my most fundamental interests, however, let me develop clarity what kind of career I could become happy with in the long-term and, therefore, ignited a new guiding light. In the context of where I want my career to develop, it is mainly two insights which emerged from these highly inspiring eleven months.

Ever since I attended a train-the-trainer seminar back in 2010, I felt a great joy and satisfaction from delivering training sessions of all kinds and see the growth and development they trigger in their participants. While this has been part of my motivation to become a scuba diving instructor, I have also always had vague dreams of making a career within Learning & Development. However, that is where the story ended. It never passed beyond being a vague dream and I never got a clear idea of how to make it happen. Having stepped out of the professional rat race and having looked at my life from a different perspective, has now made me more convinced than ever that this is where I see myself professionally in the long-term. This clarity feels great, as it comes with a new sense of direction. Conveniently, being a trainer and coach goes well hand in hand with travelling the world, which has always been another big passion of mine. As I am still highly eager to be independent to some degree and explore new places, it comes as no surprise that during my time in Thailand an entirely new goal has grown, which had never made it to my consciousness before, despite being somehow hiddenly present in the deeper layers of my thoughts. As I got to know a lot of digital nomads and saw how much they enjoyed their freedom, I grew more and more eager to create a passive income of some kind and, consequently, become less financially dependent on 9-to-5 jobs, in which I need to ask my supervisor for permission, whenever I want to leave my hometown between Monday and Friday. While this dependence has been a normal part of my life for almost a decade, it starts to feel more and more like a too significant interference with my personal freedom. While I am currently not planning to quit working in a 9-to-5 scheme, I am convinced, however, that a decreased dependence on such a job can play a significant role in achieving peace of mind.

This dream of financial and geographical independence has been part of my unconscious thoughts already before and I dare to say that many people around the world share this dream. However, like most other people except for a rare minority of digital nomads, I always lacked the ideas how to make it happen and would never have had the courage to go the necessary steps. I had to take a step out of my traditional mind-set to find inspiration in Ibiza and Thailand. It is, therefore, no surprise that it was on Koh Tao where I started to take first steps into this direction. While I already had to realize for a few ideas that they do not work, I still have a list of things I want to try and have for now prioritized two pillars to start with. On one hand, having realized my interest into photography, I am getting more and more into how to take good pictures and post-edit the best out of them afterwards. Whereas it is far from making me financially independent, it has already earned me the first few Euros on stock photography platforms and provides for an interesting hobby at least. On the other hand, I am working on another pillar of my strategy right at this moment. While a big part of my motivation to write this book emerges from digesting and appreciating my experiences, I am of course hoping to publish it once finished, even if it will only earn me a small amount of money. After all, I am aiming for nothing more than making it part of my overall strategy to make a part of my income passive. And let us face it... Sitting in the sun and putting some of the greatest experiences of my life onto paper does not at all feel like work.

While these new initiatives relate to my life outside scuba diving, I have also found a new motivation to progress my diving career. While my development as a scuba diver seemed to have come to an end, as I had achieved my biggest goal, I am now more ambitious than ever. I have become more convinced of my dream to own stakes in a dive centre, have started to think about progressing until Instructor Trainer and already took steps to extend my scuba diving experience into entirely new areas, as I have signed up for my first course for diving in overhead environments. It feels great to engage on a course as a student again after being on so many courses as the instructor. It fills me with a lot of satisfaction to realize how much inspiration these eleven months provided for my future. It is obviously a long way to achieve these goals, but my journey from my Advanced Open Water Diver course in 2015 to where I am now proved so powerfully that everything is possible, if only we accept that everything starts with the first small steps and do not withdraw from our dreams in the absence of immediate results.

It was this newly gained clarity on my mission and some new goals which made me ready to end my sabbatical in spring 2020. As mentioned on some earlier pages of this book, I was offered a new job in November 2019, a few days before I flew to Thailand. When the time for my decision had come at the end of 2019, I delayed the decision to the point that I risked the company would withdraw from their offer. Looking back in retrospective now, it becomes obvious that this procrastination resulted from me being afraid of getting sucked back into a mediocre life without any real perspective. As soon as the abovementioned ideas had appeared in my mind, however, I was ready to sign the contract, as it no longer felt like the end of a journey. Now it felt like a good decision to secure the financial stability necessary to prepare for the next big steps.

After all, I am now more convinced than ever that this is what life is all about. It is not about the destination, but it is the journey itself that matters. It is about doing what feels right at any given moment and while I am afraid of going back into my old life just to feel like having reached a dead end, it feels right to take a step to build up some more financial stability. In this context, my mission has provided me inner stability and has felt like a save harbour, irrespective of how it has been positively or negatively influenced by this side-track. In the end, this is exactly what a clear mission is supposed to provide. It is supposed to keep us on track and act as a guiding line amidst the turbulences which life inevitably provides, while it is in no way meant to be a restrictive force. Therefore, it has unfolded its true power to keep me aligned with my higher interests, motivations, beliefs and paradigms when going one of the greatest and most beautiful side-tracks of my life. It has enabled the integration of this adventure into a greater whole. Nevertheless, the synthesis was bi-directional. Not only worked my mission statement as a guiding light, but also did my detour provide unbelievably valuable and necessary challenge and inspiration for my well-established way of thinking.

The Inuit have a saying that no time is lost when you go a detour, as life still goes on. This belief has left a lasting impact on my mindset, ever since I read it many years ago. While it is not meant to populate irresponsibility, it describes so powerfully the idea that life is not meant to take us somewhere but meant to be the meaning itself. If there is one learning for me to take from my eleven months in Ibiza and Thailand, it is the insight that detours are where life unfolds its beauty. After all, my very own detour has not only provided me a great time, but also enriched my long-term life in many aspects. It has not jeopardized any of the pillars for what is commonly seen as a successful life and I have not lost anything I had before, as I am for example back in a well-paid job and the relationship with my family is better than before. On the contrary, I have now finally started to work on some of my longest held but neglected dreams, for example writing this book. Therefore, my detour has not only added life into my lifetime, but also given me the necessary energy to stand up for my true beliefs. Being the owner of my very own personal mission statement certainly helps, as this is the place where these very personal beliefs are.

It has now been five months since I left Thailand and about four months since I returned to Germany and started my new job. It, therefore, appears logical to reflect on how easy it was to settle back into a normal life. At least, so it did about one year ago, when I drafted the outline for this book. However, by now I have come to understand that a reflection on what makes a life "normal" is so much more needed than a reflection on settling back into a normal life. During these enriching months in Ibiza and Thailand I had the joy to meet a lot of people, who took a much bigger step than I did. When I quit my job in 2019, I had a clear goal in mind to return after a still to be determined time. Many others embarked on their adventure without this psychological return ticket, planning to make their new "normal" what many people consider extraordinary. One year ago, I also considered life as a scuba diving instructor immensely extraordinary and maximum a once-in-a-lifetime adventure. Now I ask myself the question what justifies the idea that staring into a screen in a neon-lit office for almost 50% of our wake hours and spending a big portion of the remaining time to offset the adverse effects of doing so is any more normal than earning money with something you love and inspiring others to develop a new passion. While I have by now again got used to a stable income from a 9-to-5 office job, I refuse the idea that I have left the extraordinary behind and shall now continue living for the next 32 years what a big part of society considers a normal life. If after all the inspirations I take this one year as a break instead of a trim tab, it would turn out as a lost opportunity after all. I struggle to find any justification why society shall have the right to determine what is normal, while only we can take the very personal decision what makes us happy and gives our life a meaning. What might appear normal from one perspective, might not do so from another.

It was exactly this dilemma which caused me to procrastinate my commitment to my new job around the turn from 2019 into 2020. As I did not see a long-term perspective yet, signing up for a job in my hometown felt like a dead end and a greatly missed opportunity to break loose from my mediocre life. This gordian knot in my mind was only solved when I started to see a long-term perspective. Consequently, accepting this job offer did no longer feel like a risk to get sucked back into what I refused to see as a normal life but instead as a reasonable and necessary next leg to go towards my future goals. More specifically, it was mainly two aspects which enabled this mental transformation. On one hand, I came to realize that it would be hard to achieve my goal of becoming an Instructor Trainer abroad, as that required me to teach certain advanced courses, which I was most likely not going to teach on Koh Tao. On the other hand, getting into a serious relationship did not only make me eager to eliminate the geographical distance but also came with a feeling that life would not become mediocre again. In fact, getting together with a partner outside my hometown felt like a great possibility to continue living more adventures. Finally, my time abroad had been transformed from a time off to a trim tab towards a new life and a better future, even if that meant settling back into my old life for a while.

So, it happened that I found myself on a flight to Stockholm by the middle of March 2020 and finally back to Germany by the end of April. However, the start-up of my new life in Germany was meant to be entirely different and significantly more challenging than I expected it to be. While many new perspectives on my well-established habits and routines resulted from returning in a relationship with a girlfriend living 1,800 km away after leaving Germany having lived as a single for many years, there was one even more unforeseen and so far unimaginable factor which made it difficult to restart my social life as it used to be. When I returned home, Germany as many other countries around the globe was in full lockdown due to the prevailing COVID-19 pandemic. While shops, restaurants and alike were gradually opening again by the time when I finished my 14 days of quarantine, social and public gatherings remained to be prohibited beyond the absolute minimum. For me, whose previous social life had been centred heavily around my membership in the voluntary fire department of my hometown, this meant an unexpected difficulty to reactivate the connections with my peers, as also our common non-mandatory activities had been reduced to the absolute minimum. This adversity, however, came with the positive side effect that it was not made too easy for me to be sucked back into all my old routines, but instead I had to put some effort into finding meaningful activities for my free time. It did not take long after my return to Germany to realize how easy it is to allow all the powerful inspirations and learnings to fade away and to grow back slowly but steadily into the life that I so desperately wanted to leave behind. Therefore, the reduced social activity of the voluntary fire department managed to offset partly COVID-19's potential to be an excuse to fall back into a lazy and mediocre life.

After all, one of my greatest concerns has been and still is that my time off will turn into a simple break and that I would, therefore, miss its great potential to function as a trim tab towards an enriched life. While it used to be the vision of becoming an Instructor Trainer and working towards life as a digital nomad, which made me ready to sign my new work contract and leave Koh Tao behind, my focus has now changed and it is the work towards a life with my girlfriend that gives me a perspective and off-sets the fear of falling back into a mediocre life, as being back in my hometown does now not feel like a dead end but instead a necessary step towards the next bigger developments. I am, therefore, confident that I will manage to keep at least some of the learnings and inspirations alive and turn them into a more fulfilled life in the future. On the other hand, however, I must never forget how easy it is to fall back into old routines and habits and that I must keep pushing for a proactive lifestyle to not let myself be limited by social expectations.

Now I am typing these lines in October 2020 and am thinking about the first six months after my return, half a year which should have born the fruits from all the new perspectives of stepping off the rat race for one year. Doing so, I am asking myself the questions if it was the right time or too early to leave Koh Tao in March 2020 and how well I managed to settle back into life in Germany or, even better, how well I managed not to settle back into "normal" life. The latter is, in other words, the question how well I managed to keep my inspirations alive and change life for the better. While I could have enjoyed a few more months on Koh Tao or elsewhere in that region and typing these lines fills my heart with a great desire to go on such an adventure again, it turned out as a good idea to go home for two reasons.

Firstly, it was sustainability that drove my decision to return home. While my savings could have easily covered a few more months without any income, it still appears as a wise decision to not use all my savings and instead leave Asia behind before the low season hit and made my life in Thailand even less self-sustainable than it already was. In full denial of the "once in a lifetime" mindset, it feels so much better now to work for the financial independence to do such an adventure again in a few years without the same financial limitations and without the need to return into the corporate world at some point. After all, there is no reason not to start over again as a scuba diving instructor at the age of 45.

Secondly, if I had not taken the decision to return home in March 2020, force majeure would have taken it for me very soon, as the diving industry has been forced into a global stillstand due to COVID-19. Over the last few months, it has been shocking to follow on social media how many of even the most successful and legendary professionals within the diving business have left Koh Tao and returned to their home countries, which some of them left almost a decade ago. Hence, it appears naïve to assume that I would have succeeded as a freelancer during a time, when Thailand kept its borders closed for international tourism. Therefore, it now turns out a better decision than I could have imagined that I accepted my new job in January 2020, just in time before economy in Europe and the rest of the world hit rock bottom.

After six months back in Germany, my assessment whether my sabbatical has worked as a trim tab is twofold. While I must admit that I have re-acquired some of my old habits and ways of thinking, I dare to say that my sabbatical has become a greater enabler than I ever imagined it to become. What started as an idea of a "once in a lifetime" break has now transformed my mindset from following social expectations and spending my life working for retirement towards living unconventionally, being happy and ultimately living my life. If the original idea had become reality, I would now consider these twelve months a failed attempt to break out, while it now fills me with satisfaction to see them as an experiment that gave me a vision of an independent future life and, thus, a purpose to work and strive for in my current life.

After all, I can conclude that many of my old habits and thought patterns have come back, but some of my most fundamental paradigms have changed. It has been one of the most important learnings from my journey that there is not such a thing like a "normal" life. It is up to every one of us to define what "normal" means for them and how they want to live their life. As insights and learnings continue throughout our entire life, I do now believe that there will never be a point in life when we will be fully settled. It is up to us, however, to make our life fulfilling and constantly push ourselves away from mediocracy. It is frightening to feel the powerful strings and forces with which mediocracy is now trying to pull me back into its sphere. Thus, it is very encouraging to type these lines and feel all the inspirations and spirit return, a desperately needed reminder, as they were slowly fading away amidst all the challenges of everyday life.

7 CONCLUSIONS

It has now been 20 months since I quit my old job, 17 months since taking a one-way flight to Ibiza and 11 months since I wrote the first lines of this book 30'000 feet above the ground somewhere between Dubai and Kuala Lumpur, from where my next flight would take me to Bangkok. After all these months filled with tremendous amounts of experiences and memories it is now time to ask myself the question if I would go on such a journey again.

As already elaborated in the earlier chapters of this book, these months in Ibiza and Thailand have not always been easy and I have certainly had moments asking myself why I did not stay within the routines and comfort of my well-established life. I had moments worrying about my financial situation, longing for German food, and missing relaxed evenings with German television. Now that I do not need to worry about finances anymore and got these advantages of my well-established life back, I know the answer to this question. It requires the extra mile, a big leap out of the comfort zone and certain sacrifices to make the beauties of life flourish. Despite the challenging times in Ibiza during the peak season and the worries in Thailand, when the season was low, it has still been one of the most laid-back periods of my life and a year in which I felt as alive as I have not felt for a long time. After all, this is probably one of the most worthwhile returns for making comparably small sacrifices.

As the reader, who made it all the way to this chapter, should understand by now, this sabbatical has become so much more than it was originally intended to be. What has started as an idea of an extended break on the beach with an ambition to reconnect with myself at best, has turned into a powerful transforming force, which has given me a revived and clearer vision for the future. Not only has this journey enabled my mind to break free from the eternal hamster wheel of a 9-to-5 job, but also has it led to more specific ideas and plans than I could ever have imagined. They range from simply new passions like photography through the joy of finally writing my own book after lacking inspirations to do so for almost a decade to a potentially life-changing vision for how to become financially independent within ten years. In the light of all these beautiful outcomes, it comes easy to conclude that it was well worth overcoming the doubts and excuses discussed in chapter 3, even more so when anticipating the long-term benefits from, for instance, cutting down on my fixed costs more than I would have ever done without a need.

When I now look back on my life so far, it becomes clear that it has always been the extraordinary periods of life which have triggered the most powerful personality developments and transformations. It does not even matter if it was the consciously chosen adventures such as my exchange semester in Australia and now this sabbatical in Ibiza and Thailand on one hand, or unvoluntary extended breaks such as an operation on my knee several years ago on the other hand. Therefore, it is not hard to conclude that all these previously discussed developments like more ease when approaching people, an improved relationship with my family and taking myself less serious are direct positive outcomes of going this extra mile and seeing myself and my life from a different perspective for twelve months. Recognizing this pattern and now noticing that it took only six months for the inspirations to start fading away, it becomes self-evident how desperately important it is to break with your patterns every now and then. Since challenging my routines has once again proven so powerful to me and reminded me in such a memorable way of the importance to take unlimited responsibility for how our life goes, I am now convinced that this will not remain a "once in a lifetime" adventure but instead become a recurring part of my life.

As elaborated before, these twelve months were far from always easy. While a change of job, environment and lifestyle never comes easy, I can now identify mainly two psychological dilemmas, which were challenging but triggered some of the greatest personal developments of this time. As discussed before, it did not take long for my spirit to go down as soon as one of my biggest life goals so far had been accomplished. As my dream to become a scuba diving instructor had been the main driving force for my motivation for a long time,

I was suddenly confronted with the utter absence of a life goal and next step for the time after my sabbatical. After only a few days in Ibiza, I felt an emptiness like the one I felt after graduation from university. However, this time it seemed so much harder to solve, as I could not distract myself with a vision of starting a great career. Secondly, after years of blaming many of the flaws of my life on external conditions, it almost hurt to acknowledge that things would not automatically become better by simply changing my environment. Receiving the same feedback as before from different people made it impossible to deny that changes in my life would only be possible if I changed my mindset and habits. Here I was... Some of my most fundamental assumptions and paradigms had been shattered, as I was facing the ugly truth that I had spent years of using fake external limitations and a vision of a glorious future life as excuses to procrastinate life in the here and now.

Fortunately, in the end these dilemmas turned out as powerful as they were painful at first. Sometimes it takes the removal of metaphorical layers of dust to reveal what is hidden below, no matter how ugly it is. Without the absence of a life goal and all the excuses and distractions from my previous life, I neither would have come up with a vision for my future nor would the insights and developments described in chapter 4 have been possible. Moving out of my comfort zone created the need to take an honest look at my life. After years of striving towards a goal without any next steps after accomplishing it, now a vision of becoming Instructor Trainer and a better underwater photographer, working for a passive income and financial independence, and eventually owning my own dive centre in a few years is becoming increasingly clear. As these require an entrepreneurial mindset of some degree, I am happy to realize another outcome from stepping off the beaten track. While I have always been far from an entrepreneurial mindset, this side of me has now grown stronger because of not being able to rely on a secure monthly income anymore but instead facing a need to make sure I get along.

As it has been such a great time and at the same time enriched my thinking with so many inspirations for the better, I am now convinced that it will not remain a once-in-a-lifetime adventure. It will rather turn into a recurring concept for my life, as I am increasingly letting go of the idea of working the 40+ best years of my life and leaving all the fun for later. Therefore, it seems so much more important to ask myself the question what I should have done differently instead of asking whether I should have done it at all. The answer is simple. I should have been less risk-averse and should have gone all-in instead of the half-hearted approach I chose before my mind got ready for the big leap. My Instructor Training Course in Koh Tao in November 2018 was probably one of the most important milestones of my entire journey. I was already a divemaster when I went there, and it took me another five months after completion before boarding my flight to Ibiza. My fear of something going wrong prevented me from going all-in and fully indulging into the adventure. The whole experience and journey would have benefitted a lot from quitting my job to do a 2-months divemaster program and stay for the Instructor Training Course and beyond right away. Even my detour through Ibiza instead of going to Koh Tao as the place where I really dreamt to be, appears like going half-hearted instead of fully committing to the adventure. Ultimately, this decision was a result of my need for small steps to grow my comfort zone little by little before getting ready for the big step. After all, it often seems worth to ask ourselves the question what can happen in the worst case.

In the end, my reasons to choose Ibiza over Thailand in the first place turned out as just some more excuses to avoid taking as big a step as possible out of my comfort zone. I always explained my decision with the benefits of the European Union, the supposedly higher life standards in Ibiza and so forth. However, I have now come to understand that these were excuses to avoid what I was afraid of much more than they were actual reasons. Adversely enough, my life standards in Thailand, for instance, were higher than those in Ibiza. The result of keeping one leg inside the comfort zone, however, could have been anticipated. After the first six months, my dream felt unaccomplished and I would now suffer from dire unrest and regret if I had not spent the additional four months in Thailand. As a result, one of the main lessons to learn from this experience is to not let our fear of uncertainty or perceived social norms hold us back from living our life to the fullest. If we have a dream, we must never let excuses prevent us from accomplishing it. After all, it did not take more than a few days until I felt comfortable and at home in Koh Tao, so that my reasons to go to Ibiza were revealed as the excuses they were.

Finally, this adventure has become a story of everything being possible in life. Back in 2007 I did not even think about becoming certified as an Open Water Diver. Twelve years later I was working as a full-time instructor, doing the job of those who I admired back then. These last twelve years have taught me that we should never dream too small. In 2008 I was brainstorming about a bucket list for my life and wrote down that one day I want to go diving in the Red Sea in Egypt. I have been there twice by the time I am writing these lines, and it has certainly not been the last time. A few years later, when I started to dream about becoming a scuba diving instructor, I felt like a maniac to even only have this dream and it took its time until I dared to share this idea with the first people. Even when I was making big steps to finally becoming an instructor, there was still this inner voice which insisted that I would never have the guts to quit my job and live somewhere else in the world for some time. This inner voice only shut up once my flight to Ibiza was booked and I had quit my old job, so that there was no way back. I do not even want to imagine how great opportunities I would have missed if I had listened to all my inner voices along the way and had allowed myself to be satisfied with the initial small dreams. These last years will continue to serve as a reminder for myself about the potential of seemingly small and meaningless steps or decisions and the impressive developments they can enable in the future, if we only allow things to happen and life to drive us.

While it was easy to come up with these thoughts in the inspiring and challenging environments of Ibiza and Thailand, it is now becoming increasingly difficult to maintain this newly gained spirit, as I am back in my old life with a 9-to-5 job. In fact, it fills me with worry that I recognize many of my pre-Ibiza thought patterns to enter the stage again. My long to-do list and daily time pressure at work has started to shift my focus back from being to doing, and it gets increasingly difficult to drop this toxic mindset in my free time. As I notice how the bubble, which has been holding me back for so many years, slowly starts to build up around me again, I start to acknowledge the dire importance of setting myself a goal again and developing a vision for the next step. Comparing the development of my mindset over the last years, it is painful to understand that it is slowly getting back to the point where it used to be by the time when I flew to Ibiza. Thus, I have now made up my mind that I will certainly go on more adventures again and will never again see it as the one-way road that starts after graduation and ends with retirement. After all, life has too much to offer to spend 40 years in a neon-lit office, only waiting for the day, when we can finally retire and start living our life. I am currently lacking the clear vision and goal, what this next big adventure can be, but I am sure and convinced that the time for it will come sooner or later. After all, there is a time for everything in life and it is our decision whether we want to eliminate all possibilities for magic to happen in our daily struggle to fight for the next promotion or if we want to be open and mindful and be willing to go off the beaten track, if the time is right for it. After these twelve months and all their invaluable experiences and learnings, I have come to understand that one of the greatest obstacles, which holds us back from so many good things in life, is the fear of not fitting into social and cultural expectations and norms. Once we manage to let go of this faulty and dangerous paradigm and become a truly independent person, we are ready to leave our bubble and live our life. We have then reached the true freedom to focus on our passion and purpose and do something that fulfils us instead of doing something for the sole sake of paying of our bills.

As I hope that this book is being read by many, who are going or are planning to go a similar path like me, I believe it is well worth to translate my experiences into practical tips and tricks how to make the most of this journey. I do not want those to be understood as a checklist of some kind, neither do I claim it to be comprehensive or complete, but I hope it can trigger some thoughts and let some of the readers learn from my experiences.

1. Before you take any decisions on where in the world to go, it is essential that you clarify your expectations and spend some honest thoughts on how to achieve them. There can be many different motivations to leave your life for a while and to live and work as a scuba diving instructor somewhere in the world. Living and diving in a tropical place with great diving, experiencing the joy of high-quality teaching in a high-quality dive centre, living the laid back and fun life of so many instructors you met before or getting to know lots of fun people are just a few motivations that jump into my mind right away. As their accomplishment depends so much on the location and dive centre you choose, it is critical that you know what you want upfront and probably equally important that you do not fall into false assumptions or stereotypes. As elaborated earlier in this book, one of my reasons to choose Ibiza over, for instance, Egypt was the assumingly

higher lifestyle... An assumption that turned out entirely false, as I had much more amenities in Thailand than in Ibiza! This clarification of expectations should also include a few thoughts about what kind of customers you want to teach. In Ibiza it turned out that I was mainly teaching families and children, while in Koh Tao I got to teach backpacking young adults on an around-the-world trip as the kind of customers I was really interested to teach.

2. Even though you are probably going to have a good time, you should not expect a glorious lifestyle no matter what. You should not forget that, despite all the fun, scuba diving instructor is after all a job and, as in every job, there is probably going to be a boss who decides over who you teach, which courses you teach and how many hours a day you work. And let us face it... Besides a lot of fun students there will also be those who will give you a hard time. While it is a job that guarantees a lot of fun and satisfaction, it would be naïve to believe that it will always be pure joy and never stressful. There are tanks to be carried and filled or equipment to be maintained behind the scenes, so that long days are the rule rather than the exception. Especially in the Mediterranean you may want to be prepared for at least six days with around 50 hours per week, as it is typically seasonal work with an according high pressure to earn twelve months of income in six months of work. It was one occasion in Ibiza that

visualizes this stereotype and the reality quite well. I was approaching 40 hours that week, when the week was by far not over yet, and was on a constant struggle to have the time to consume enough water and food, when I was texting with a friend how he was doing. One can imagine that his response "All good in life, but probably not as relaxed as yours" to my question about his well-being got me a little irritated. Unless you want to go freelance, as I did in Koh Tao, you will probably be working more than you will be hanging out on the beach. As full-time and freelance both have their disadvantages and benefits, I am going to elaborate on the two options in more detail in the next point.

3. Before you make any arrangements, make up your mind whether you want to work full-time or as a freelancer. As I have experienced (and in some way enjoyed) both, I can now see the benefits and disadvantages of both. Being full-time employed in Ibiza gave me a sense of security, as I knew what I was going to do the next six months and I did not have to worry about the next steps. Working as a freelancer on Koh Tao, on the other hand, did not provide me that sense of security, as I never knew when the next job opportunity would arise. Planning was impossible, as jobs for the next day mostly arose after 5 p.m. However, it came with a sense of freedom, which I had not experienced for several years, as I could theoretically decide which jobs to take. If I felt like a short trip to Singapore or

Vietnam, no one would stop me, which was quite the opposite to Ibiza, where I could not even decide which days I would take off from the annual leave, which I was legally entitled to. In the end, the decision for full-time or freelance should match your personality and preferences for freedom versus security. Surprisingly enough, I felt more peace of mind in Ibiza than in Thailand despite all the stress, since I am a person who appreciates structures and routines. Consequently, the open-endedness and freedom on Koh Tao was a direly needed challenge and new perspective, which however made me feel at unrest a lot in the beginning. It started to feel great, however, when my mindset started to change from doing to being.

4. The previously discussed clarifications of your expectations and whether to go full-time or freelance should go along with some idea of how long you want to go. I am far away from advocating that you should fix a specific period right away, as I believe that keeping it open-ended to some degree is important to experience the right peace of mind and spirit. However, some thoughts about the time frame seem important, as they can influence your destination and arrangements at home. Most Mediterranean dive centres require to commit to six months, as that is how long the season lasts in that region. Whenever I was speaking to dive centres in Egypt or the Maldives, however, they expressed their strong preferences for twelve

months' contracts. Besides the availability of options where to go, the duration further can have an impact on which arrangements you make at home. When I left for Ibiza, I decided to keep my apartment, despite not being allowed to sublet it, and to unregister my car but keep it in storage, so I could register it again upon my return. What seemed to be the best decisions at that time, as I was planning for only six months, may have been decided entirely different, if I had already known that I would be gone for almost twelve months. The longer you plan to go, the less "packages" to worry about at home you may want to keep.

5. Make your life lean to increase your flexibility and freedom! As discussed earlier in this book, free yourself from unnecessary financial, materialistic, and organizational burdens! It will increase your available cash significantly, if you take an honest look at your fixed costs and cut the unnecessary ones that are only existing, as it was comfortable to keep them. You may even be surprised, how many payments for insurances or pension funds you can pause for a certain time without significant negative impacts. A similar honest look can also be useful on your materialistic belongings. You should neither underestimate how much financial buffer you can generate by selling the things you never use, nor should you overestimate the amount of baggage you need to carry with you on your journey. After all, being away for one year does not

necessarily require much more baggage than being away for 14 days, as you cannot take one set of underwear per day anyways. Finally, if you manage to make your organization lean and your life paperless, you have already gone a big step towards being independent and free. Having been overly organized for many years, it has been a relieving experience for me to not possess a printer in Ibiza in Thailand, so I had to learn to not get nervous, if I am not printing flight tickets, for instance.

6. You should not underestimate what it takes to be surrounded by people on vacation all the time. Meeting laid-back and happy people was one of my main motivators to go on this journey in the first place. This expectation has been fully met and I am grateful for all the fun and interesting people I met along the way. However, as the rather introvert person I am, it has also been a challenge to be constantly surrounded by people and let go of a great deal of privacy. On one hand, it is important to be ready to meet many people but in most cases wave goodbye after only a few days. Building lasting and deep relationships should, therefore, not be your main expectation. On the other hand, you must not forget that people around you will be on vacation, while you are there to work. They will want to go out, party and have a good time, while you need to get out of bed for work the next morning for a job which is certainly physically exhausting. What may work for a few days in a row,

will certainly lead to a need for a break at some point. However, I have experienced what it takes to justify a single alcohol-free day with proper sleep in six months, as most customers will never see the fact that you have been going on for weeks – "But come on… we are just here for one week. How can you think about sleeping now?"

7. You should not be too romantic when planning your journey. Do not forget that also scuba diving instructor is first and foremost a job, even if it is a highly rewarding and fun one. You need to be prepared to also get into the water when you do not feel like it at all or when the visibility is close to zero and be aware that you will not be able to cherry-pick your students. While most of them are fun and rewarding to teach and hang around with, there will certainly also be those that will remind you why you are getting paid for your job. And as it happens with most things, which we do repeatedly, you will probably also appreciate the diving less after some time. I can, therefore, only recommend that you remind yourself every now and then what a privileged life you are living. It came as a great epiphany to me one day on the beach of Koh Tao that my alternative would be to sit in a neon-lit office staring into a computer screen 40 hours a week. When you plan to turn your hobby into your profession, you should also think about what to do with your free time, if it exists. A little change to scuba diving every so often will help to maintain

your appreciation for your job and, consequently, increase your overall satisfaction.

8. Do not expect quick success and be prepared that it may require persistence and patience to become successful in this industry. It can be commonly read on social media how easy it is to complete an Instructor Training Course (and eventually pay a little extra for an internship afterwards) as a fast track into a successful career as a scuba diving instructor. While the diving industry has been in need for more instructors until the rise of COVID-19, "from zero to hero" may still not be realistic. I made the experience that the Mediterranean region may be a good place to get work for the inexperienced instructors and set foot into the industry, while the chances are little to get well-paid jobs in regions, where dive centres can afford to cherry-pick their staff. I received replies from dive centres in the Maldives, for instance, who refused to even talk to me until I had 800 logged dives. Koh Tao with its vast number of dive centres appeared as an easy place to find work as well, but also here I had to face the reality that it takes patience and a lot of freelance jobs, before dive centres consider you for full-time employment. It took me around three months until I was on some kind of short list at some dive centres and was one of the first instructors who they asked if they were in need for freelancers. I learnt three things on Koh Tao. First, it would have been naïve to aim only for

the prestigious dive centres with the biggest boats. It was usually the smaller dive centre who were more promising in terms of jobs. Second, having established contact and taught a successful course does not mean you can relax. Even after a few courses for some dive centres it happened that the next one went out on job boards and I did not get approached. It takes a constant effort to not get forgotten in a job market, where people come and leave all the time. Third, it cannot harm to have some financial buffers when you start. Unless you already have a permanent job secured upon arrival, as I had in Ibiza, there will most likely be a period with little or no income to cover, until the diving becomes sustainable.

9. Make you sure to clarify your principal expectations towards your break upfront in terms of what you want to achieve. Simply wanting to have a good time and leaving the rat race of a corporate life to reset your peace of mind may let you make entirely different decisions than wanting to develop your scuba diving career. I am an SSI instructor but spent my six months in Ibiza working for a CMAS dive centre. Consequently, I was not teaching on my own behalf and certifying my students myself but was doing so under the direct supervision of the dive centre's owner and leaving the certifications to him. This setup did neither appear as a problem when I took the decision, nor did it influence my quality of life during these six months. However, I

noticed after some time that it started to bother the goal-oriented part of my personality a lot, as it felt like wasting half a year in terms of career progression. Reaching higher development levels within SSI depends on teaching a certain number of certain course types, which I did practically do in Ibiza, but they were obviously not eligible for higher instructor ratings within SSI. Therefore, it felt like a great relief to start teaching eligible courses in Koh Tao.

10. You should be ready to accept that you will mainly be teaching beginner courses. Before leaving for Ibiza, I qualified myself to teach five more specialty courses within SSI, hoping that I would also be able to teach them during my sabbatical. In the end, however, they did neither make any difference in Ibiza as I was anyways teaching CMAS nor in Thailand, as it did not take long to realize that I would mainly teach Open Water Diver, Advanced Adventurer, Try Scuba and, if lucky, Stress and Rescue. The reason was simply that the typical tourist does not seem to bother much about specialty courses but wants to get into diving and have a good time. While this fact did not impede my joy and fun, I had to acknowledge that it would be hard to reach my goal of becoming Instructor Trainer in Koh Tao, since that requires to teach certain courses, which are almost impossible to get assigned as a freelancer. So, I came to understand that, if I wanted to progress my scuba diving career,

I needed to return to teaching in Germany at some point.

11. Having written about goal-orientation in the previous two points, it is maybe worth to mention that too much goal-focus can impede your fun and satisfaction. I can only strongly recommend that you get ready to let go and live in the moment and do not think too much about the next steps. While it cannot harm to have an idea about what is going to happen after your sabbatical, going with the flow and allowing life to go its way was one of the greatest outcomes for me and turned out as one of the most important mindset transitions for really indulging into a relaxed and laid-back lifestyle. After several years in the corporate world, where tight deadlines and a high level of organization are inherent parts of a project manager's work, it came as one of the greatest reliefs in my life so far, when that mindset was slowly fading away.

12. To get the most out of your journey it is highly recommendable to walk off the beaten tracks as much as possible. Commuting between your apartment, your dive centre and the most common beach bars and restaurants, can be an easy way to a great time, but you may look back afterwards and realize that you missed out on some of the most authentic experiences. In Koh Tao it was usually when departing from the main touristic roads into apparently shady and suspicious neighbourhoods, where I found the hidden treasures. I intentionally

wrote "apparently" in the previous sentence, since it is only our European and influenced-by-Hollywood mind that instantly connects dirty roads and simple houses with no-go areas. However, in less developed places, where most of the great diving takes place, it is the standard for many people and does not impede their hospitality and friendliness. In fact, some of the crappy-on-first-sight restaurants, which may not seem recommendable after reading too many tourist guides, turned out as the best places for lunch and dinner. Not only was the food usually much better, but also was it drastically cheaper than in the mainstream tourist restaurants on the main roads. No surprise that these were the places where you would meet most of your fellow dive professionals and long-term residents. And let us face it... If a place is busy from many customers, it is not only a good sign, but it also means that it has a high turnover of ingredients, so that the likelihood of food poisoning is comparably low.

13. When preparing for your adventure, it cannot harm to spend some time thinking about some practical arrangements. Even though you will be abroad for a while, people will try to reach you by post. Getting the post forwarded may not be practical depending on the location. It turned out highly convenient for me that the postal service in Germany offered the opportunity to scan my post and send it to me by email, while the physical post

was sent to my parents' place in a bulk once a month. To generate some free cash flow, it certainly makes sense to critically check which fixed costs are needed. It did not take me long to identify several magazine abos which I could quit and even some insurance or pension funds could be put on hold for a while, with a minimal impact on the later payments but a significant impact on my cash flow now. See it as a great opportunity to break with some of your habits and clean your life for a time that will span much longer than your sabbatical.

14. While you should not allow planning for the time after your sabbatical to impede with being free and enjoying life for a while, it can certainly help to have some plan in the drawer that you can take out. It can even be a good idea to account for some contingencies in case everything goes wrong. I am far from populating that you should go through life worrying about what goes wrong but being a little prepared cannot harm. It certainly makes sense to define a limit to which you want to stretch your finances before you return to your old life. Not having any savings on a remote island when the job market for whatever reasons worsens can put you into a tricky situation easily. It is easy to use my final days on Koh Tao as a perfect example. Due to COVID-19 the diving industry in Thailand came to almost an entire stillstand. The job market for freelancing dive instructors seized to exist from one day to the next. Being on Koh Tao without enough

money to book a flight home or, even worse, to pay the next visa run could have led to substantial problems. As far as I heard afterwards, the Thai immigration authorities granted exceptions to those not able to leave the country before their visas expired, but this is certainly nothing you should gamble with. Of course, no one could have anticipated COVID-19 for their contingency plans, but it was a perfect example how some financial reserves and jump-off criteria can certainly be useful.

15. Be prepared to live a simple life for a while and make sure to clarify your expectations also what comes to, for example, your accommodation. Often accommodation for dive professionals is provided by the dive centres, but do not expect it to be luxurious. Rather expect the opposite and be ready to ask the right questions when you get the chance for an interview before your employment. What may be sold to you as a room or apartment on the beach, may turn out as not much more than a simple bed under a more or less waterproof roof. While a simple lifestyle for some time can certainly be an enriching experience, it can turn out as a significant stress factor, if your accommodation does by far not meet your expectations and you need to share it with others when privacy is important for you. Allow yourself to be a bit critical when something sounds just too perfect.

16. To make your sabbatical one of the best times of your life, make sure to appreciate the things you have. Many humans have the tendency to take the things they have for granted and miss the ones they do not have. You should try to let go of that habit as much as possible. Remind yourself regularly that you are earning money with something you are passionate about and that you are living in a location where others go for vacation! You should not give in to longings and desires to easily. I missed my apartment in Germany, my German television and German food a lot when I was in Thailand. Life did, however, not get better when I got it back. In fact, one of the first things I started to miss back in Germany was the simple and easy life in Thailand, which I had never appreciated before. Make sure that you enjoy your life as it is and ask yourself if your life will really become better if you give in to your longings and desires!

17. And finally... Be open to allow your sabbatical to take the right place in your life! Do not only see it as a once-in-a-lifetime adventure but be open to let it become the eye-opening and life-changing experience it deserves to be! Avoidance to see it as an escape from life and instead accepting it as an inherent part of your new lifestyle makes it much easier to go back to a 9-to-5 job for a while if need be. Knowing that you can always go back to a laid-back lifestyle, if your finances allow, makes a lot of things much easier than having to deal with the

assumption that this was it. Returning to a "normal" life afterwards and forgetting about all the good things would be just a too big lost opportunity to change your life to the better. When I started my year off, I was thinking in a separation between my "normal" life and my extended break, while I have now come to understand that it does not have to be like that. Instead, it seems like a much better way to happiness and satisfaction to re-define your sense of "normal" and not let societal expectations limit your life choices. The only limit should be your creativity and your willingness to make things happen. "Normal" should be defined by what makes you happy, but not by what others think how you should live your life. This book has become a powerful tool for me to keep my reflections and insights alive and to make sure that I do not just fade back into my "normal" life despite having experienced this beautiful trim tab.

Now it is your time to leave your bubble and dive into blue depths!